Praise for *Actualized Leadership*

"The *Actualized Leader Profile* is the most impactful leadership assessment on the market today. If you take your results to heart and commit to personal development, it will transform your leadership style and your life."

—Cathy Bessant, *Chief Operations and Technology Officer*, Bank of America

"The framework and approaches detailed in *Actualized Leadership* provide anyone – whether you are early in your career or a seasoned leader – with immediate ways to take action for personal improvement, while prompting thoughtful reflections on what drives you, as well as how you can be better on the job and in life."

—Kathie Patterson, *Chief Human Resources Officer*, Ally Financial

"*Actualized Leadership* is the leadership book I've been waiting for. With his insightful and readable style, Sparks uncovers how a deep understanding of our motivation and experiences can help us reach our full potential as leaders and human beings."

—Jonathan S. Halkyard, *President and CEO*, Extended Stay America

"Will's approach and framework will provide you with immediate insight and the self-awareness necessary to become a more effective and resilient leader."

--Steve Clifford, *Head Coach,* Orlando Magic

"The *Actualized Leader Profile* eliminates the ego-drive rejection of typical assessment tools because each participant self assesses. The concept is brilliant as one only has to look in the mirror to confront the source of the feedback."

--Dr. Susan Sweeney, *President*, GGB Bearing Technology

"In *Actualized Leadership* Dr. Will Sparks has cemented his reputation as one of the country's foremost experts on leadership. As a former senior government executive, I value the path to personal improvement described so meticulously his work. Whether for government or business, this timely book should be required reading for those navigating the challenges we all face in our daily lives."

—Dr. Jack Caravelli, *Visiting Professor*, University of Oxford, Former *White House National Security Council Advisor*

"Anyone who is currently in a leadership position or aspires to lead an organization will benefit from Will's insight. Becoming a self-aware leader with true perspective is impossible without the proper framework. *Actualized Leadership* not only provides the framework, but also the tools that will allow you to unlock your ultimate potential as a leader."

—Peter M. Guelli, *Chief Commercial Officer*, New York Giants

"In *Actualized Leadership* Will provides a comprehensive yet simple framework for immediate insight. Using a combination of theory and expert interviews he not only makes a compelling case for why you should strive to be an Actualized Leader, he shows you how to get there."

—Kim Henderson, *Senior Vice President and Chief of Staff*, Novant Health

"Will's *Actualized Leadership* framework provides crucial insights into what drives leaders, teams and organizations, and creates a roadmap for alignment and integration that is essential for personal and organizational effectiveness."

—Peter C. Browning, *Managing Partner*, Peter Browning Partners

"There is no better assessment tool or framework on the market today for developing leaders and improving team dynamics. Without question, the personal insights you will discover with the *Actualized Leader Profile* will take your individual leadership and team performance to new heights."

--Ken Walker, *Partner*, Falfurrias Capital Partner

"The Actualized Leadership framework serves as the foundation for our executive leadership programs and Will's approach has created great results with our current and future leaders. *Actualized Leadership* allows you to focus on the critical attributes necessary to realize your leadership potential."

--Timothy Craven, *Executive Vice President*, Human Resources, JELD-WEN Inc.

"The insights and concepts presented in *Actualized Leadership* are a fantastic extension of Will's wonderfully unique ability to articulate what highly effective leadership is, and how anyone can move from where they are to where they want to be."

—Ralph H. Groce III, *Senior Vice President and Chief Information Officer*, Everest Re

"There is no greater learning experience than having a guide who is both brutally honest and detailed about his own failings, while providing evidence-based insight and advice about how to reach a new level of growth as a human being. Dr. Sparks delivers both, and he has written a book I recommend to anyone who wants to be a better person and build a better world."

—Dr. Eric B. Dent, *Professor and Uncommon Friends Endowed Chair in Ethics*, Florida Gulf Coast University

"A solid framework and strategy is fundamental to achieving a goal. In *Actualized Leadership*, Sparks delivers a simple process that enables personal and professional growth for every level of leader."

—Dwayne Black, *Senior Vice President and Chief Operations Officer*, Shutterfly

"*Actualized Leadership* is a great framework for individual and team development. Will's approach is both insightful and easy to apply. I recommend this book to anyone who is interested in becoming a better leader and creating a stronger team.

—Brent Cagle, *Chief Executive Officer*, Charlotte Douglas International Airport

"As leaders and as individuals, we are all capable of achieving more when we understand our true motivation and potential roadblocks. Will has great enthusiasm for helping people achieve their full potential and in *Actualized Leadership*, he provides a straightforward framework for doing just that."

—Eric Creviston, *President of Mobile Products*, Qorvo

In *Actualized Leadership*, Will has given us a powerful framework to decode leadership and ourselves. It will challenge you to seek answers to questions you might rather ignore, but are absolutely critical for discovering your purpose and living at your highest potential.

—Stephen C. Montague, *President and Chief Executive Officer*, Midrex Technologies

ACTUALIZED LEADERSHIP

Meeting Your Shadow & Maximizing Your Potential

ACTUALIZED
LEADERSHIP

Meeting Your Shadow &
Maximizing Your Potential

William L. Sparks, PhD

BETTER WORKPLACES
BETTER WORLD™

Society for Human Resource Management
Alexandria, Virginia | shrm.org
Society for Human Resource Management, India Office
Mumbai, India | shrmindia.org
Society for Human Resource Management
Haidian District Beijing, China | shrm.org/cn
Society for Human Resource Management, Middle East and Africa Office
Dubai, UAE | shrm.org/pages/mena.aspx

SHRM, the Society for Human Resource Management, creates better workplaces where employers and employees thrive together. As the voice of all things work, workers and the workplace, SHRM is the foremost expert, convener and thought leader on issues impacting today's evolving workplaces. With 300,000+ HR and business executive members in 165 countries, SHRM impacts the lives of more than 115 million workers and families globally. Learn more at SHRM.org and on Twitter @SHRM.

Library of Congress Cataloging-in-Publication Data
Names: Sparks, William L., author.
Title: Actualized leadership : meeting your shadow and maximizing your
   potential / William L. Sparks, PhD.
Description: First edition. | Alexandria, VA : Human Resource Management,
   [2019] | Includes bibliographical references and index.
Identifiers: LCCN 2019012959| ISBN 9781586445683 (pbk. : alk. paper)
| ISBN 9781586445706 (epub) | ISBN 9781586445713 (mobi)
Subjects: LCSH: Leadership.
Classification: LCC HD57.7 .S69425 2019 | DDC 658.4/092--dc23 LC
record   available   at   https://catalog.loc.gov/vwebv/search?searchCode
=LCCN&searchArg=2019012959&searchType=1&permalink=y

Printed in the United States of America
FIRST EDITION
PB Printing 10 9 8 7 6 5 4 3 2 1   61.19302

Table of Contents

List of Tables and Figures

Tables

Figures

Foreword

O ne of my all-time favorite movies is *The Legend of Bagger Vance*. The film's main character is a supremely gifted professional golfer named Rannulph Junuh, who is consumed by the shadows of a tragic life experience. As a result, he has been knocked off life's course; he has lost his game. His caddy, Bagger Vance, has decided to journey through the torturous dark valley with him. Unbeknown to Junuh, Bagger is committed to helping him reach his full potential, acting as a personal sage. During a poignant moment in the movie, Junuh finds himself alone in the dark shadowy woods after shanking his ball off course. In this moment, he is consumed by the flooding memories of the tragic past that has haunted him for years. Trembling in terror, he leans over to pick up his ball, preparing to give up, to quit once and for all. Then, seemingly out of nowhere, Bagger emerges and asks the question, "You going to be wanting a different club there, Junuh?" Stunned by his caddy's presence, Junuh responds, "I can't do this," and he goes on to say, "You don't understand." Bagger responds, "I don't need to understand. There ain't a soul on this entire earth that ain't got a burden to carry that he don't understand. You ain't alone with that, but you have been carrying this one long enough. Time to go on, lay it down . . . time for you to come on out of the shadows, Junuh. Time for you to choose."

In *Actualized Leadership,* Will Sparks is also asking you to choose, to come out of your own darkness and choose to reach your optimal potential. To do so, Sparks argues that we must confront our own shadow. We must move past our own tragic past and get back on the course of our life's purpose in pursuit of our own personal why. Heavily influenced by Swiss psychologist Carl Jung's concepts of individuation (the process of actualizing our ultimate potential) and the shadow (the unconscious and often irrational aspect of our own personality that is triggered under stress), Sparks challenges us to look at the dark side of how we show up as leaders. He will encourage you to step out of what Jung referred to as your "fog of illusion" and to stop blaming your troubles on others, to come out of the shadows and realize your highest potential. *Actualized Leadership* acts as a personal sage, much like Bagger Vance, but through the words of a book.

Grounded in the seminal theoretical foundations of such authorities as Jung, Abraham Maslow, Mihaly Csikszentmihalyi, David McClelland, and Viktor Frankl, *Actualized Leadership* provides a synthesized framework grounded in twenty years of research and inquiry. The book argues that individuals are represented by one of three positive motivation needs and their resulting styles: *Achiever*, *Affirmer*, or *Asserter*. Each leadership style has a unique corresponding *leadership shadow*—Fear of Failure (Achiever), Fear of Rejection (Affirmer), or Fear of Betrayal (Asserter)—which often produces less-than-optimal results, if not outright dysfunction, under stress. Sparks reminds us that we have a choice: we can choose to meet and process our shadow, or we can ignore or deny it, and it will process and manage us. Drawing on the wisdom of Viktor Frankl's notion of paradoxical intent, he argues that the more we let the fear underlying our leadership shadow drive our behavior, the more likely we are to experience the very thing we are trying to avoid: failure, rejection, or betrayal.

Much has been written on leadership and positive psychology over the past decade, with many organizations strongly embracing the notion that we must focus on people's strengths rather than their weaknesses. These organizations believe that the creation of a positive working environment encourages everybody to be their better selves. In *Actualized Leadership*, Sparks takes us a step beyond this notion. He argues that focusing only on our strengths while excluding, denying, or projecting our shadow is only one-half of the self-awareness equation. He challenges us to spend time discovering our deep, personal reason for what we do. He then moves beyond the accentuation of positive motivations and encourages us to charge into our own internal disturbances as a basis to overcome the influence of our unconscious leadership shadow. In doing so we are able to unshackle ourselves from the dark side of our own egos to ascend toward the pinnacle of our higher selves, our actualized potential.

Years ago, my mentor taught me that my primary responsibility as a catalyst for human development is to hold up mirrors to others so they can see themselves more vividly. In some cases, this reflects the sheer hidden brilliance deep inside of an individual. In other cases, it magnifies the brutal truth of how an individual's shadows show up for others. As a chief talent officer, I have found that both of these practices are essential for leadership growth. We must uncover the hidden potential in others, and we must also challenge others to deal with their repressive egos. In *Actualized Leadership*, Sparks goes even further. He does the unthinkable. He turns the mirror around and openly shares the brutal realities of his own leadership journey as a testimony to others so that they can choose.

This choice has perhaps never been more important. In today's world, more than ever, leaders need to enable resilience in their organizations. This journey begins by looking in the mirror. We live in the era of disruption, where the lack of agility is the kiss of death. John Chambers, chairman emeritus of Cisco, said that "if you don't transform . . . if you don't reinvent yourself, change your organization structure; if you don't talk about speed of innovation—you're going to get disrupted. And it'll be a brutal disruption, where the majority of companies will not exist in a meaningful way 10 to 15 years from now." A study from Washington University predicts that an estimated 40 percent of today's S&P 500 companies will no longer exist a decade from now (Ioannou, 2014). This reality leaves organizations with a critical choice: adapt or die. To do so, organizations truly need actualized leaders, leaders who can see beyond their own egos and help the organization face the tough realities of a changing world. This means that leaders must first face their own demons and charge into their leadership shadow. Tragically, my personal experience is that leaders want all the glory of leading without the cost. Few leaders are willing to pay the price necessary to charge into their shadow and do the deep work required for leading resilient, adaptive organizations. For those of you who choose to do so, those of you who are willing to plunge into this journey for the sake of your institutions, *Actualized Leadership* can serve as your sage in your own personal moments of doubt and frustration in the darkness.

—Michael J. Arena, PhD
Chief Talent Officer of General Motors
Author of *Adaptive Space*
www.adaptivespace.net

Preface

*A*ctualized Leadership is about you and your development. Although this book is written primarily for a business audience—specifically, leaders in organizational settings—its central message of how to unleash, or *actualize,* your potential is a message that any reader seeking personal transformation will find relevant and life changing.

Actualizing your potential requires balancing two seemingly contradictory states: honesty and objectivity about your current state, as well as imagination and passion for a desired future state. You must be willing to make a strong commitment to seriously pursue your own unique development and growth pathways. The Actualized Leader Profile I've developed is the culmination of more than twenty years of research. It provides a scientifically valid and reliable method to accurately assess both your strengths and limitations. This book will support your effort to develop an even deeper, more encompassing degree of self-awareness.

At some point, assuming I do my job effectively, you may feel discomfort or even irritation with this process. If that happens, we've both done our jobs. True self-awareness is not always comforting or validating; it sometimes disturbs and disrupts. However, this disturbance pushes us to find reservoirs of strength that help us reach our highest potential, leading us to transform ourselves and our relationships with others. This ultimately awakens us to new ways of leading and living.

Actualized Leadership is the first published research-based book to put into practice Abraham Maslow's highly influential theory of human motivation—specifically his concept of self-actualization—within the context of an organizational leadership setting. Through scientific analysis, I've identified nine specific traits that characterize the unique way self-actualized leaders think, feel, and act. Years of personal research in the field of organizational and leadership development have revealed a compelling business case for why self-actualization is so essential to your success as a leader. As you develop and enhance your self-actualization, you'll feel more satisfied and inspired as a leader. You'll also achieve better results and create a more engaged and effective company culture.

This book gives you the opportunity to directly apply the models and concepts of self-actualized leadership to yourself. As you work your way through the pages you will build your unique Actualized Leader Profile (ALP) report that you can use to guide your transformational journey. As with any roadmap, you'll be able to choose where to begin and end your journey. This flexibility allows you to dive into the sections that are most applicable to your specific needs for leadership development.

Many of my participants have told me that going through the development program benefited their personal lives as much as, if not more than, their professional lives. The fact is that you simply cannot separate leadership development from personal growth. Human growth, which is foundational for individual development, occurs when someone changes his or her internal belief structure. This type of growth takes place when, for example, as the result of a 360-degree assessment a person gains a new, profound insight that then leads to a significant shift in the way she sees herself, and others, which leads to personal transformation.

While leader styles, shadows, and the 9 Attributes of Actualized Leaders discussed in this book are based on years of quantitative research and scientific validation, many of the insights and suggestions come from qualitative interviews with some of today's most respected and successful leaders. They include former Bank of America Chairman and CEO Hugh McColl and Episcopal Presiding Bishop of the United States the Most Reverend Michael Curry, among others. These leaders eagerly shared their knowledge and straightforward, no-nonsense wisdom based on years of diverse experience in a wide variety of industries. The leaders who have so graciously given of their time, energy, and expertise for this book are, in alphabetical order:

» John Allison, retired Chairman and Chief Executive Officer, BB&T
» Carl Armato, Chief Executive Officer, Novant Healthcare
» Cathy Bessant, Chief Operations and Technology Officer, Bank of America
» Jeff Brown, Chief Executive Officer, Ally Financial
» The Most Reverend Michael Curry, Presiding Bishop, The Episcopal Church
» Pamela Davies, PhD, President, Queens University of Charlotte
» Hugh McColl, retired Chairman and Chief Executive Officer, Bank of America
» Mike McGuire, Chief Executive Officer, Grant Thornton
» Fred Whitfield, President and Vice Chairman, the Charlotte Hornets

My personal view is that anything you haven't accomplished in your professional life up to now is due in large part to what I call your *leadership shadow*. Famed Swiss psychologist Carl Jung coined the term "the shadow" to describe the dark, negative qualities of an individual that are activated under stress. These qualities are often the counterpart to the many positive attributes we possess and embody. Through this book you will have the opportunity to meet and process your leadership shadow so that it does not process and manage you, releasing you to achieve your highest sense of calling and purpose. The ALP is a tool that helps you accurately identify and own your leadership shadow. The Actualized Leader Profile, to be completed online, is your essential resource and companion throughout the book. The most challenging part of the journey will be to stay out of your own way. As you read, consider the cost of not managing your shadow and then assess the price you will continue to pay until you finally decide to meet, and integrate, it.

In the end, this book is about helping you find affirming and self-actualizing experiences more often and about showing you how to feel them more intensely. I can assure you that if you fully engage in this process, complete the ALP assessment honestly and accurately, read and consider the suggestions in this book, and commit to following through with your development, you will be a more effective, happy, and satisfied leader. Consequently, you'll create a more engaged culture for your colleagues and associates. And you'll create a more satisfying life at home.

Acknowledgments

There are a number of people I would like to thank for their insight, creativity, and support over the years in general, and in writing this book in particular. First, my business partner John Repede has been a tremendous colleague over the years, and his combined grasp of statistics and creativity with technology is without equal. I want to thank my colleagues at Queens University of Charlotte, especially Pamela Davies and John Bennett, for their ongoing support. I owe a debt of gratitude to my friends at EnPro Industries for their interest and support over the years, especially Steve Macadam, Robert McLean, Susan Sweeney, Gilles Hudon, Bill Favenesi, Marvin Riley, Eric Vaillancourt, and Jon Rickers.

I want to recognize and thank my business partners Erika Weed and Jane Williams for their commitment to our work, and to this project. Thanks to Stump Design for their creative input and design excellence. Mark Morrow and Linda Vespa provided tremendous editorial support. I appreciate Mark reminding me that I did not need to use twelve words when four would suffice. Linda, thank you for your careful attention to detail, and for your patience with my consistent mistakes!

A number of folks have provided support and input over the years, including Bob Freese, Kayshia Kruger, Michelle Shail, Maura McGrath, Yeshua Perez, Craig Hopkins, Anderlei Cortez, Peter Macon, and Anna Esther Mason. Many mentors and business colleagues have helped shape my thinking, and my writing, and they include Jim Long, Jerry Harvey, John Lobuts, Peter Browning, and Ken Walker.

I especially want to thank Matt Davis and Montrese Hamilton with SHRM's book-publishing program for their tremendous support and encouragement.

Finally, I want to thank my family and my wife Erin for their ongoing love and support.

Dedication

This book is dedicated to Dr. Dominic J. Monetta, my mentor, colleague, and dear friend. You taught me more about actualizing potential than anyone else.

Special Introduction

I am pleased that Will asked me to offer my own personal perspective on human development as an introduction to *Actualized Leadership: Meeting Your Shadow & Maximizing Your Potential*. Please allow me to start by disclosing that I am by no means an expert on human development. I have never been formally trained in this extensive field, nor do I have any credentials to put forward. I only know and believe it to my core—that every human being is equally worthy, full of perfect goodness and good intention at their most innate and basic level. This was either taught to me by my father or was inborn, because it has been part of me since I can remember.

This foundational belief shapes my perspective of the world so much that I have been coached over the years that I am "too naïve," "too trusting of others," "not discerning enough of others' motives," and the like. I fully accept that feedback; however, I believe as one grows up in our imperfect world, their inborn goodness gets corrupted, twisted, or distorted by the ego-driven aspects of our society and those of other people. Unfortunately, people don't actually behave perfectly. All of us are left to wrestle with our own imperfectness as a lifelong struggle of growth and development in an attempt to more closely align our internal self with the external self we desperately want others to see.

My second foundational belief is that all human beings are built for learning. (I tend to use the terms "learning," "growth," and "development" interchangeably.) It's easy to recognize in young children, harder to recognize in adults, and particularly hard to recognize in adults who appear to have given up on their own growth. But I believe that *everyone* still has the internal flame of motivation to grow, no matter how dim the light has become.

Therefore, my two foundational beliefs about you (and everyone) are that you are inherently good and that you have an innate desire for learning and growth.

If these characteristics are true of everyone, why then do some people seem to grow and develop on an accelerated track while others stagnate? I have observed in myself and others that much of the reason has to do with the mechanics or process that we follow. Let me offer a simple conceptual model to illustrate the two common approaches to development that I have experienced and also observed in others. Frankly, one works and the other doesn't.

The conceptual model is a simple *why* → *what* → *how* framework. Every person has their own *why*, which can be thought of as their purpose for living. It's the answer to the question "Why are you here on this earth?" Some of you will know the answer. Others have yet to discover it, or it is still emerging, and some have a general sense of the answer but it is not fully clear. I believe that discovering one's true why at the fundamental level, and living into it, is a lifelong pursuit. At EnPro, we spend a significant amount of time working on each of our whys.

A person's why leads to a *what*, either explicitly or subconsciously. This what can be thought of as what one chooses to do with their time, both in the present and in the future. This can be applied to one's profession or education as well as choices in their personal life; it is how one chooses to allocate time in all the various aspects of their life.

One's what then finally leads to the *how*. This is how one acts in the world and toward others. For example, it's the difference between listening and talking, telling and coaching; being patient and impatient, compassionate and cold-hearted, trusting and suspicious; and the like. This why → what → how model serves as the guiding framework for the two very different developmental paths that I have observed.

Let me start with the one that has not worked for me and, I daresay, I have not seen work for others. It is the direct shift from one's current how to a new and better how, without the connection to purpose. "I want to shift from being a poor listener to being a good listener," "from cold-heartedness to compassion," "from uninspiring to inspirational as a leader." In my history, I have wanted to change many undesirable behaviors (hows) to better behaviors, only to see my well-intended and earnest efforts fail as I fell back into old, familiar patterns. It's easy for me to describe better behaviors, but it has proven very difficult to consistently achieve and sustain them. I believe the answer lies in the process. The mechanics actually matter! I believe they make all the difference.

The process that I have found to work much more effectively takes a different path in the why → what → how framework. While meaningful data from self-assessments and 360-degree feedback are an essential starting point, they are not sufficient. At least, they have not been sufficient for me. While any developmental process must start with an accurate self-assessment, it's not enough to use this self-knowledge as the primary motivation to live differently.

Using honest and frank self-understanding to fundamentally, truly shift behavior requires a process that anchors in a person's why. I was never disciplined or adept enough to use my self-understanding to directly make a real shift. I had to travel through what I was spending my time on and, more fundamentally, my purpose. I had to shift at the level of my "why." Only after connecting deeply with my why could I then clearly see *what* I should do with my time and then translate that into *how* I wanted to behave toward others. Through deeply understanding my purpose, I am able to continue holding myself to a standard of behavior that is consistent with my purpose.

My old why had too much to do with my own career—making myself noticed or trying to convince others I was special. I needed and deserved recognition! I had to show what I could do, to prove that I was successful, I was smart, and I was worthy. These were the unspoken motives, my old why. This motivation was subconscious. I had never really contemplated my true purpose.

As a part of my journey, I shifted. Moving away from an Asserter style, which is focused more on personal power, to an Actualized Affirmer style, which is focused more on others, allowed me to more deeply connect with my true sense of purpose. Informed by my deepest source of spirituality, I believe that my purpose lies in service to others. I committed myself to helping others grow and develop and also to accepting help from others. At this point in my life at EnPro, our formal corporate purpose is "The full release of human possibility," and we operate with a dual bottom-line philosophy. Our operating model puts profit and human development on the same level of importance. As we produce and deliver the best possible engineered products for our customers, we want our employees to release their full potential and flourish as a result.

So when I fall into my old counterproductive behaviors, which my team will tell you happens on a regular basis, I work on myself by connecting to my new why of guiding the creation of a company committed to releasing human possibility, and I use that to guide what I spend my time on and how I behave toward others.

This book presents the best leader-development assessment and personal-growth tool that I know of today. I'm confident you will find it enormously valuable to better understand your own ego mechanism and leadership shadow. My hope for you is that you will also work to find your own why and use it to anchor your path for growth and achieving your highest potential.

—Steve Macadam, CEO, EnPro
Industries Inc.

Part I
Meeting Your Shadow

Chapter 1
My F in Life

What's in This Chapter?

» A Lesson in Self-Awareness
» Finding Professional Lessons in Personal Relationships
» Introduction to Actualized Leadership
» What's Next

People will do anything, no matter how absurd, to avoid facing their own soul. One does not become enlightened by imagining figures of light, but by making the darkness conscious.

—Carl Jung

Self-awareness is foundational for both leadership effectiveness and personal growth. Most of the time we confuse self-awareness with knowing, and playing to, only our strengths. We usually try to ignore or deny our negative qualities and instinctual reactions; that is why we often resort to blaming others or defending our own limitations when under stress. Swiss psychologist Carl Jung referred to this common reaction as the "shadow" and famously said that blaming our troubles on others instead of truly facing ourselves condemns most of us to live our lives in the "fog of illusion." Think of the shadow as the Mr. or Mrs. Hyde that is the counterpoint to our very best or actualized self, our Dr. Jekyll. When we're under stress, tired, lonely, or "hangry"—or after a cocktail or two—our shadow is more likely to emerge, or erupt.

The good news is that you have a choice: you can either process and manage your shadow, or it will process and manage you. The former is painful but necessary in order to reach your highest potential. The latter is much easier because we don't have to face ourselves and our shortcomings, but ultimately, it's much more disruptive as it usually results in a bad ending: a demotion, termination, divorce, and the like.

Jung's concept of the shadow is crucial to the points I make in this book and also, most importantly, to your ability to make the needed changes in your life (including the development of true self-awareness) to transform and maximize your leadership potential. Without this recognition, it is hard to chart a clear path forward because in a contest of wills, your shadow nearly always wins. It's a truth I had to learn the hard way.

LEADERSHIP SHADOWS

The term "leadership shadow" describes one of the three fear-based reactions we have under stress. Based on the seminal work of Carl Jung and his concept of the shadow, leadership shadows correspond to each of the three motive needs that drive our style: *Achiever—Fear of Failure; Affirmer—Fear of Rejection; Asserter—Fear of Betrayal.* By assessing your dominant motive need, the assessment included with this book (http://www.ALPFree.com) will give you greater insight to both your style and your leadership shadow. In addition to this enhanced self-awareness, strategies for identifying your leadership shadow triggers are provided to help you more effectively manage your leadership shadow and, in doing so, actualize your highest potential.

A Lesson in Self-Awareness

Dr. Jerry B. Harvey was one of the most insightful and enigmatic thinkers in the fields of organizational behavior and management. Although he died in August 2015, twenty years ago he had a profound impact on my life when I was a graduate student at The George Washington University (GW). In fact, his theories, models, and frameworks ("musings" or "sermons" as he called them) still influence me today.

Anyone lucky enough to have known or worked with Jerry realized early on that he was a walking contradiction. He was fiercely intelligent, but he spoke with a slow, deliberate, Texas drawl. He was a "Bible-thumping Southern Baptist" (his words) but also irreverent as he examined spiritual issues such as "The Organizational Dynamics of the Last Supper and Why Judas Was Not a Traitor" and made the analogy between leading organizational change and passing gas, or "Tooting Your Own Horn," in church.

Jerry referred to business organizations as "Phrog Farms," yet he was in constant demand to consult with business leaders and give keynote addresses. He often reminded us that when we get stabbed in the back, "Our Fingerprints Are Usually on the Knife." He claimed that it was immoral to give someone objective feedback and more ethical to have "Prayers of Communication" with them. He condemned the "Tragedy of the No-Nonsense Manager" and stated time and again that leadership creates loneliness, which then leads to "anaclitic depression" and, if not remedied, a much shorter life. He compared leaders who participate in reductions in force just for the sake of profits to Adolf Eichmann, and he encouraged "Future Managers to Cheat" if that meant giving and receiving help.

Jerry's classic book *The Abilene Paradox* is a dry, funny, and insightful reminder that it is our "inability to manage agreement, not conflict, that is the single most pressing issue of modern organizations." But despite the apparent contradictions in his writing and professional relationships, there was love and encouragement behind his approach, especially with his students. Jerry constantly reminded his students to push outside their comfort zones, to think with more rigor, to write with greater precision, and to have the courage to ask and seek the answers to big and often painful questions about life and its purpose. I know of no other writer or professor so insightful and provocative. In a world of sound bites, social media updates, and tweets, we need his existential musings and irreverent sermons now more than ever.

Dr. Harvey was my professor for the first time in 1996 when I began GW's doctoral program in Organizational Behavior and Development. As a freshly minted graduate with a master's degree in psychology and management, I was excited to continue my studies under the famed author of *The Abilene Paradox.*

My first class with Dr. Harvey on group dynamics was unlike any class I had ever taken before. Students wrote poems, performed songs, and played musical instruments to illustrate their understanding of the theoretical models of small group behavior and change dynamics. I was too insecure at the time to do something so creative, so I decided to write a final paper about my divorce and the dysfunction of dependency. I thought it was an excellent choice since the topic of dependency had been the basis for Dr. Harvey's dysfunctional dynamic explored in *The Abilene Paradox.* I worked hard on the paper, and when I turned it in I was confident that I had done a respectable job of it.

During our last class, all the other students got their final project grades except me. Instead, he singled me out for special attention. "William," Dr. Harvey said as he stared at me over the top of his glasses. "Son, you're going to need to come see me for your grade." To say I was shocked to be called out in front of the whole class is more than an understatement!

The next day I knocked on Dr. Harvey's half-open office door and peeked in. He had his back to me and was reading his Bible. Without looking up, he pointed to an empty chair in front of his desk. I sat down and nervously fidgeted in the chair while waiting for him to acknowledge me. Eventually, he closed the Bible, rubbed his eyes, and turned around to look directly at me. "Well, William," he said, "what do we need to talk about?" Clearing my throat, I responded that I was there to talk about my paper. "Wrong," he said.

Surprised, I quickly reassessed the meeting's purpose and tried another response. "Well then," I replied, "I must be here to talk about my experience in the class, right?"

This response brought both irritation and amusement. "Son," he said, "let me be very clear with you: I don't give a damn about your experience in my class."

"We're going to try this one more time, William, before I fail you," he told me. "Son, what are we here to talk about?" Now I was nervous and, thinking I had nothing to lose, finally let my guard down and ventured another guess.

"I am here to talk about my divorce," I replied.

He grinned just a bit. "I'll give you a B- on that response. No, son, we're here to talk about you," he said, directly pointing a finger at me. "So, tell me, how the hell did all of this happen?" I assumed "this" meant my divorce, so I repeated the details of it that I had discussed in the paper. Essentially, I blamed my ex-wife for the divorce because she changed and became too needy and dependent. Dr. Harvey listened intently, nodding occasionally and often grimacing.

When I finished with my sad tale, Dr. Harvey said he was very sorry. He also said he would be praying for me and for my ex-wife. He was also ready to pray with me. "William," he said, "I've got some good news and bad news. The good news is that you made an A on the paper. It's well researched, thoughtful, and well written." He said that I intellectually understood the dysfunction of dependency, even well enough to teach it one day. Now I felt better, and it occurred to me (arrogantly of course) that the real reason he'd invited me to his office was because he didn't want to embarrass the other, mostly older, students with this glowing feedback. But he quickly put an end to those fantasies.

"But here's bad news. The bad news is that I'm giving you an F in life," Dr. Harvey told me, skewering my ego. "Son, I am of the professional opinion that the only thing more dysfunctional than a codependent, which is your soon-to-be-ex-wife, is a prodependent, which is you. You created this dynamic. I bet you had to make every decision. I suspect you had to solve every problem. I bet you had to have the last word in every argument. And, I'd bet that you were always *right*. Now you want me to feel sorry for you, but I don't. Not at all. I feel sorry for her."

In the span of a few seconds I had gone from feeling proud and invincible to feeling defeated and hopeless. Then he expressed in very direct, colorful language that he really resented my coming into his office and trying to manipulate him into feeling sorry for me, telling me that I was "in way over [my] head." He was very angry and strongly suggested that I never, ever do that to him again.

Then he really schooled me.

He said that if I truly wanted to learn something during my time at GW—and, by the way, do the rest of the world a big favor—I should spend the next four or five years figuring out how my own failings led to my divorce. His final words to me as I left his office were along the lines of this: "William, I'm going to level with you; I doubt very seriously you're going to graduate from this program. You've gone through life never getting out of third gear, and you'll never get past me unless you're in overdrive, assuming you even have an overdrive.

"And, to make matters worse," he continued, "you have a South Carolina chip on your shoulder. That alone will make it virtually impossible for you to be truly open and receptive to the prayers I plan to have with you. But, if you take the next few years and figure out why the hell you did that to her, you'll get your money's worth from the program whether you graduate or not."

With that parting shot, he turned his back and continued reading his Bible. I spent the better part of that evening being angry, castigating the "great" Dr. Harvey. I went out with a few friends for drinks and engaged them in a pity party. My friends sided with me, of course, but deep down I knew that Dr. Harvey was right. The next morning, something *transformational* happened as I finally admitted that what happened in my marriage was largely my fault and that many had suffered because of my actions. It was a bitter pill to swallow, but I soon discovered that taking personal responsibility allowed me to feel truly awake and engaged in my life for the first time.

Finding Professional Lessons and Personal Relationships

Of course, Dr. Harvey gave me a real gift that day. He forced me to face my own shadow and take responsibility for my actions. You may have a similar story you can recall, when someone forced you to examine your motives, take responsibility, and face down your own shadow. If you've experienced such a cathartic event, you will recognize the following important lessons that I drew from my schooling from Dr. Harvey.

1. Feedback is a gift.

   Jerry could have treated me differently and not been so blunt; his feedback really hurt because it was spot on. It was the first time anyone had shown me my own shadow. Jerry saw that I was sad and broken, and vulnerable. He could have told me to hang in there and that everything would be fine. But instead, he told me the truth without worrying about my reaction. My lesson from this experience is to never sugarcoat the truth. When we do this to someone, our dishonesty dishonors them. The ultimate expression of love and respect is to provide candid, direct feedback. Doing so honors the recipient and offers the real possibility of transformation.

2. You are responsible for what you say, not for how the other person responds.

   Jerry honored me by not really caring how I might respond to what he told me. We often base our feedback on how we think someone will respond. That is a totally misguided approach. A watered-down version of the truth instead of the hard, cold truth might be met with a positive reaction, but the outcome is mostly ineffective. By intentionally detaching yourself from someone else's reaction, your candor liberates you to be a true agent of change.

3. Personal growth and transformation happen only when we have the courage to face our shadow.

   We may desperately want to make a fresh start or move forward, but our repeating behaviors always give us the same unsatisfactory outcomes. Jung did not believe in fate. Instead, he believed that what holds us back are our shadows, always patiently waiting to thwart our best intention to move on. Jung is often credited with saying that we "meet our destiny on the road we took to avoid it." Even though it is painful and uncomfortable, introducing someone to their shadow is the only way to help true growth and lasting change.

In the twenty-plus years since my encounter with Jerry, I have retold this story many times. My intention is to help others take responsibility for their lives and liberate themselves to live up to their ultimate potential. Feedback is indeed a gift. And even though the exchange with Jerry was very painful, it was ultimately the most precious thing anyone has ever given me.

A month before Jerry passed away, we traded emails. He let me know that he wasn't doing well, but he had the *My "F" in Life* blog printed and posted above his desk. When I told him how much he had meant to me, his response was classic Jerry Harvey: "William, for God's sake you should know by now that I take no credit for any growth you may have experienced during your time with me, nor any blame for future regression."

Rest in peace, Dr. Harvey. I suspect your musings are keeping your heavenly neighbors on their toes, and in stitches.

Introduction to Actualized Leadership

A comprehensive framework for the Actualized Leadership model is provided in Chapter 3, but I want to provide an introduction and overview now to anchor the material in Chapter 2. If you have not yet done so, I encourage you to complete the free assessment includ-ed with this book, the Actualized Leader Profile (Short Form), here: www.ALPFree.com or text WILL SPARKS to 36260 to download the free app.

After you submit your responses, you will be taken immedi-ately to your profile results that will provide a leader style sum-mary and estimation of your current degree of self-actualization. (Please note: If you would like to complete the full version of the ALP, which includes scores for all three motive needs and leader styles, your current degree of self-actualization, and your score on both the 9 Attributes of Actualized Leaders and the 3 Sequences of Self-Actualization, please visit www.DrWillSparks.com/ALPoffer.)

The Actualized Leadership model is based on assessing your dominant motive needs. There are three distinct motive needs that drive our behavior and leadership style: achievement, affiliation, and power. Each motive need predicts a specific style of leadership, and each corresponds to a distinct leadership shadow and behav-ioral tendencies. Table 1.1 provides an overview and summary of the Actualized Leadership model. A comprehensive overview of the framework, including a summary of the theoretical components of the model, is outlined in Chapter 3.

In addition to the three leader styles and leadership shadows, the framework discusses the characteristics, or attributes, of actualized leaders. Whether you are an Achiever, Affirmer, or Asserter, the goal is to become actualized in your style so that you can more effec-tively manage both the frequency and the intensity of your leader-ship shadow. Based on years of research and quantitative assessment (see Appendix C), the Actualized Leadership model identifies nine characteristics of self-actualized individuals, what I refer to as the 9 Attributes of Actualized Leaders. These nine attributes are orga-nized in three domains: cognition (how actualized leaders think), emotion (how actualized leaders feel), and behavior (what actual-ized leaders do). There are three attributes in each domain, resulting in a total of nine. Connecting together one attribute from each of

Table 1.1. Summary of the Actualized Performance Framework

Leadership Style	Motivation	Description	Leadership Shadow	Shadow Tendencies	Impact on Others
Achiever	Achievement	Organized, Focused, Disciplined, Detail-oriented	Fear of Failure	Narrow-minded, Rigid, Cautious, "Micromanger"	"Detached" Group Culture
Affirmer	Affiliation	Friendly, Warm, Empathetic, Loyal	Fear of Rejection	Anxious, Conflict-avoidant, Naïve, Accommodating	"Dramatic" Group Culture
Asserter	Power	Candid, Decisive, Rational, Strategic	Fear of Betrayal	Controlling, Arrogant, Blunt, Condescending	"Dependent" Group Culture

the three domains results in a "sequence" of self-actualization. The 3 Sequences of Self-Actualization are Confidence, Performance, and Renewal. Table 1.2 provides an overview of both the 9 Attributes of Actualized Leaders and the 3 Sequences of Self-Actualization. Both of these concepts are discussed in great detail, and each attribute includes an interview from an organizational leader, in Part III of the book (Chapters 5–8).

What's Next

Many who consider themselves self-aware acknowledge and play only to their strengths, without ever fully considering their impact on others. Chapter 2 offers an overview of the many internal and external distractions in modern life that often prevent us from being truly self-aware and inhibit our growth and ultimate attainment of our highest potential. The chapter offers practical suggestions for helping you truly grow in your self-awareness so that you can step into your highest potential.

Table 1.2. Nine Attributes of Actualized Leaders

Three Sequences of Self-Actualization	COGNITION How Actualized Leaders Think	EMOTION How Actualized Leaders Feel	BEHAVIOR What Actualized Leaders Do
CONFIDENCE	**1. OBJECTIVE** The degree to which your judgment is based on the facts and is not influenced by personal feelings.	**4. COURAGE** The degree to which you are willing to do something that frightens you.	**7. CANDOR** The degree to which you are open, honest, frank, and sincere in your communications with others.
PERFORMANCE	**2. HYPERFOCUS** The degree to which you consistently engage in an intense form of mental concentration.	**5. TRUST** The degree to which you are willing to maintain a confident expectation in others.	**8. FLOW** The degree to which you consistently engage in peak performance.
RENEWAL	**3. OPTIMAL TIME ORIENTATION (OTO)** The degree to which you have a balanced sense of time and live primarily in the present.	**6. ACCEPTANCE** The degree to which you totally and completely accept yourself.	**9. SOLITUDE** The degree to which you are comfortable being alone.

Chapter 2
The Myth of Self-Awareness

What's in This Chapter?

» Today's Assault on Self-Awareness
» The Secrets You Keep, Keep You
» On Becoming a Walking Contradiction
» Actualizing Your Highest Potential
» What's Next

Who looks outside, dreams; who looks inside, awakes.

—Carl Jung

We are the only species on the planet with a known capacity for self-awareness and reflection. Author, researcher, and UCLA professor of psychiatry Daniel Siegel characterized this unique ability to reflect on what we are thinking, how we are feeling, and why we act in a certain way as "mindsight." Unfortunately, becoming a self-aware human being is a challenging assignment given our shadows' ability (as noted in the previous chapter) to compel us to live in a fog of illusion. Perhaps it is why psychologist Abraham Maslow said that less than 10 percent of us truly actualize (or fully realize) our highest human potential.

That's far too few of us gaining benefits from a deep, profound self-awareness. We should strive to be "the awareness *behind*" our thoughts and emotions, as world-renowned contemporary spiritualist Eckhart Tolle says, "rather than *being*" these thoughts and emotions. Such transcendence is open to everyone, not just gifted artists, writers, and athletes, if we are willing to be vulnerable and meet our shadow (see sidebar).

TRANSCENDING YOURSELF

We catch glimpses of greatness when we see individuals who transcend what's considered "normal" human ability. For example, you might be inspired by the story of Jack Nicklaus's improbable, and unforgettable, comeback on the back nine at the 1986 Masters Tournament in Augusta, GA.

Or perhaps you see such transcendence in Michael Jordan's extraordinary performance during the 1998 NBA Finals, despite total exhaustion and a debilitating case of flu that would have stopped any other player. The same dynamic applies to artistic endeavors. Consider Meryl Streep in one of her more than twenty Academy Award–nominated roles or Rush's drummer Neil Peart (or Geddy Lee or Alex Lifeson for that matter) playing "Tom Sawyer."

The performances by these and other artists and performers often leave us with the impression that their reach is farther than the normal reaches of human ability. You may find yourself enamored with a certain writer when you become lost in his or her world. And most, if not all, of us can recall at least one time in our lives when everything went our way and our almost effortless responses were met with success and exhilaration. If you have experienced this feeling, you've felt the power of self-actualization.

I believe leaders instinctively want to *look inside* to find this powerful knowledge, but they lack a comprehensive tool to help them get beyond their own fog of illusion. In large measure, providing that tool is the precise purpose of this book.

Distractions That Keep Us in the Fog of Illusion

Every journey begins in optimism, and this one is no exception. Unfortunately, it is easier to think about facing down our shadows, getting past Jung's fog of illusion, and moving on to become an

Actualized Leader than actually doing the work to make it happen. Why is that?

First, we live in a StrengthsFinder culture that confuses knowing your strengths with being self-aware. Yes, playing to your strengths is critical to optimizing personal effectiveness, but getting comfortable with your limitations, deficiencies, and importantly, what happens to you under stress . . . now that's more difficult. Knowing your strengths and playing to them is important, but it's only one-half of the self-awareness equation. Besides, psychological studies consistently show that individuals overestimate their strengths and underestimate their weaknesses. One of the primary aims of this book is to help you transcend any pretense of self-awareness and performance to help you take an honest, objective look at both sides of the coin, good and bad.

Another roadblock to becoming an actualized leader is our reluctance to ask for feedback—good or bad. Instead, we build a facade that emphasizes our talents so that we won't feel the sting of criticism. But we discover, sometimes too late, that our defensive wall is a prison that blots out the insight and feedback we need to grow into our fullest potential.

A third roadblock is the deadly blame game that allows us to build an entire support system of family, friends, and colleagues who agree with our every complaint, observation, and insight. Rarely, if ever, does this support group stop us in the middle of our latest carping to say, "Maybe it's you, or maybe it's your fault." As Jerry Harvey reminded me during our "F in life" discussion, his job was not to collude with me. He guessed that my family and friends had done that enough. Rather, his job was to confront me with reality, whether I liked it or not.

Finally, our journey to self-actualization can come to a dead stop with our self-deception, a human ability that Socrates said "is the worst thing of all." John Allison, retired chairman and CEO of BB&T Bank, says that there is only one unforgivable sin in leadership: evading the truth. When we ignore or diminish constructive feedback or criticism because it conflicts with our ideal or ego, we take a step away from reality. Actualized leaders have the discipline and the courage to confront reality, even when it hurts.

Deception Has Never Been Easier

Unfortunately, life in the hyperconnected twenty-first century makes self-deception easy. We have smartphones, iPads, and social media to help keep us perpetually distracted. We often pay more attention to our Facebook status than to our own growth and development.

The world's best leaders clearly know their own strengths and weaknesses, and they use this knowledge to actively manage both the bright side and the murky dark side of their personas. Self-awareness has long been considered a foundational pillar of exceptional leadership and personal effectiveness. Daniel Goleman's (1995, 2002) *Emotional Intelligence* model and Peter Drucker's (2008) support for the "technology of self-awareness" are just two examples.

Maslow implored us to be courageous and live outside our comfort zones, but habit, fear, and the comfort of "good enough" often get in the way. The recognition that we must get past this roadblock to self-actualization has spawned an entire self-help industry populated by motivational speakers and enlightened gurus promising a quick fix. Books abound as well and include Napoleon Hill's (2005) *Think and Grow Rich* and Rhonda Byrne's (2006) *The Secret*. However, just thinking positive thoughts won't result in self-actualization.

The fact is, without making a commitment to self-understanding and getting comfortable with your shadow, the journey is unlikely to end in a positive outcome. This book demystifies the concept of self-actualization, especially as it applies to organizational leadership, while honoring the spiritual and deep human connection that is indeed a part of this exploration.

The Secrets You Keep, Keep You

*Secrets act like a psychic poison that alien-
ates their possessor from the community.*

—Carl Jung

We all have private thoughts, feelings, and interests that we may not share with anyone, even with those closest to us. However, actively kept secrets (things that might hurt or embarrass us or others) can become a destructive part of our shadow and prevent us from achieving our higher self. Below is a brief examination of these concepts and how to break free from their influence and the internal prison they create.

Private vs. Secret

Privacy is the state of being unobserved. It can include our deepest values and beliefs as well as our daydreams and fantasies. We may choose to reveal these beliefs and thoughts at some point and, in doing so, create a more intimate relationship with someone else. A secret is something we actively hide because some degree of fear or shame is associated with it. We fully believe that revealing the secret might harm or embarrass us or others. As a well-known tenet from Alcoholics Anonymous states: "You're only as sick as your secrets."

Benefits of Disclosure

Revealing a secret to someone—whether it's confessing your discomfort with an inappropriate behavior you keep overlooking or a colleague's incorrect assumption about what motivates you at work—must be done with care. However, the personal and professional rewards can be great. Here are a few rewards of such disclosure:

1. Confessing a secret may open the door not only to forgiveness from others but also to truly forgiving yourself. It's an important benefit, especially as it relates to this

book, since forgiveness is the third and final step in the Transformational Change Cycle we'll discuss in Chapter 9.

2. Confessing avoids compounding the hurt, disappointment, and betrayal that others feel when a secret is revealed to them by another source.

3. Confessing may be liberating and connect us to others in meaningful ways. Coming clean frees you from an emotional burden and allows for deeper, more meaningful relationships.

The decision to reveal or hide a secret depends on the situation and the risk. However, you should consider Jung's caution that keeping secrets is like drinking psychic poison: it alienates us, not only from others but also from our highest, actualized self.

How much poison have you consumed in your life? Is it time for some cleansing in the form of transparency and authenticity with someone special in your life? What destiny might become available to you on the road of disclosure?

Leaders must be willing to confront and accept the secrets contained in their leadership shadow to achieve their true leadership potential. Tragically, a leader's denial of their shadow will give it unyielding power over them.

On Becoming a Walking Contradiction

Better to be whole than perfect.

—Carl Jung

If someone referred to you as a "walking contradiction," how would that make you feel? Before I studied Jung and Maslow, it would have made me feel embarrassed and probably angry. I would have associated that phrase with inconsistency or disingenuity, the opposite of desired qualities like reliability and authenticity that had been ingrained in me from an early age. I suspect that many of you reading this would feel the same way. And we would both be wrong.

I hope that by the end of this section you will see the phrase "walking contradiction" as a wonderful compliment highlighting that you are, in fact, actualizing to your fullest potential by integrating your shadow. Now let's examine common contradictions that leaders confront and explore strategies that will help you integrate these paradoxes into your nature and ultimately exhibit more consistent leadership behaviors.

The Yin and Yang of Leadership

In the prestigious journal *Academy of Management Perspectives*, Waldman and Bowen cited three principal paradoxes that leaders in organizations face and offered some practical tips to effectively manage them. These paradoxes include the need to:

» Exhibit a confident sense of self . . . while projecting humility.
» Maintain order . . . while letting go of control.
» Sustain continuity . . . while pursuing necessary change.

The notion that leaders must learn how to live with these paradoxes is not new. Almost fifty years ago authors Robert Blake and Jane Mouton introduced the Managerial Grid (today known as the Leadership Grid), which directly discussed this contradiction. The foundation of their seminal model posited that leaders normally concern themselves with at least two contradictory expectations in the workplace: *concern for people* and *concern for production*. Blake and Mouton concluded that leaders who directly engaged with both these workplace realities were the most effective.

Author Paul Hersey in his book *The Situational Leader* expanded on this grid model and offered a Situational Leadership framework that accounted for the attitude and capabilities of the followers.

(Famed leadership guru Ken Blanchard also took up the situational leadership cause in his 1999 book *Leadership and the One Minute Manager: Increasing Effectiveness Through Situational Leadership.*) Still, even with this refinement, the competing tensions between people and performance continue to impact the eventual outcomes and decisions made in the workplace.

Contradiction and Creativity

Creative problem-solving, innovative thinking, and perspective-taking strategies are hallmarks of a self-actualized leader. However, such creativity is not necessarily a natural asset for leaders and is more associated with gifted artists of all kinds. Mihaly Csikszentmihalyi, who conducted his seminal work on the topic of flow, also conducted ground-breaking work in the area of creativity. Csikszentmihalyi found the following puzzling contradictions in the creative process. According to his research, creativity requires the following:

» High energy and the ability to be quiet and still.
» Being smart and being naïve.
» Being disciplined and being playful.
» Being realistic while embracing fantasy.
» Being proud and being humble.

Importantly, Csikszentmihalyi found that creative individuals are comfortable with their sometimes-quirky personalities and their individual creative rhythms (e.g., a preference for working in the morning or the evening and when to sleep or take their meals). These creative individuals also love what they are doing and do not necessarily count as their primary professional driver financial success or fame. Rather, creative people do what they do because they genuinely love their work.

How would your direct reports describe your style? Are you a creative leader, or a destructive one?

Actualizing Your Highest Potential

The last twenty years of research into self-awareness and leadership effectiveness have led me to two simple but profound truths:

1. The more you fear something, the more likely you are to experience it.
2. If you don't manage this fear (your shadow), then it will manage you.

Actualized leaders don't say daily affirmations or think exclusively positive thoughts to attain this higher emotional status. No, their success lies in the simplest but, for many, the most challenging requirement of the journey: the courage to be truly honest with yourself. Leaders who effectively manage their fears, including the fear of self-knowledge, are less reactive, more responsive, and ultimately more resilient.

Actualized leaders have characteristics that set them apart from other leaders. The good news is that these characteristics—the 9 Attributes of Actualized Leaders—can be developed by anyone willing to implement the strategies and embrace the suggested exercises and techniques found in this book.

The difficult news is that you must face and acknowledge your shadow by taking a deep dive into the pool of your own self-awareness. That's a tall order if you've spent a lifetime ignoring, denying, or projecting your own deficiencies onto others. The truth is that you cannot hide from this showdown. Ultimately, and when you least expect it, your shadow will force a confrontation.

Your leadership shadow is right there, and believe me, most of the people in your life are aware of it (whether you know it or not). So why don't you do yourself and your colleagues, friends, and family a favor and begin to manage your shadow? The positive effects will cascade beyond the impact on your own life, transforming your circle of influence as well.

The framework I've created to help you achieve this goal is built on an integration of the seminal works of our most influential thinkers on human motivation, self-actualization, and leadership. It is helpful to remind yourself occasionally that your inward reflection will lead to outward improvements and effectiveness that will manifest as a more productive external reality and increasingly authentic interactions with everyone you meet.

What's Next

Chapter 3 provides a summary and introduction to the theoretical framework for actualized leadership. From Viktor Frankl's philosophical insights to David McClelland's and Abraham Maslow's seminal works on human motivation, the chapter pulls these strands together to present a comprehensive framework for leader development and personal growth. The foundation for the model is the work of Carl Jung, who, in addition to introducing the concept of the shadow, was instrumental in influencing David McClelland's research into individual differences and motive needs, as well as Maslow's concept of self-actualization, what Jung referred to as "self-realization" and "individuation."

Part II
Leadership and
Organizational Dynamics

Chapter 3
Actualized Leadership: A Framework

What's in This Chapter?

» Carl Jung: Individual Differences, the Shadow, and Individuation
» David McClelland: The Three Motive Need Drivers
» Abraham Maslow: Self-Actualization
» Viktor Frankl: Personal Freedom and Paradoxical Intent
» What's Next

The Actualized Leader Profile (ALP) is designed to integrate various and sometimes competing models of human behavior as they relate to leadership behaviors. The models and their theoretical foundations are presented in this section along with linkages to a group of renowned psychologists, researchers, and human development philosophers including Carl Jung, David McClelland, Abraham Maslow, and Viktor Frankl. The ALP combines these models and theories into an integrated framework. Although Abraham Maslow, who coined the term "self-actualization," is the cornerstone for this book's perspective on human potential and peak performance, the framework is largely grounded in the work of the famous Swiss psychoanalyst Carl Jung.

Carl Jung: Individual Differences, the Shadow, and Individuation

One could argue that Swiss psychiatrist and psychoanalyst Carl Jung has influenced Western culture more than any other single individual in the last one hundred years. For example, his theories on personality types (introversion and extroversion) underlie one of the most widely used personality-assessment tools in the world, the Myers-Briggs Type Indicator (MBTI). In addition, his theories about the shared structures of our unconscious mind (what he called the "collective shadow") and his writing about archetypes (the notion that all civilizations draw meaning from shared, universal symbols) have dominated philosophical debate about human civilization for generations. Moreover, his concept of synchronicity (what he called "meaningful coincidences") has redefined psychotherapy practice and research.

One of Jung's noted pupils, Henry Murray of Harvard, went on to apply Jung's interest in individual differences by explaining human behavior from a motive need perspective. In turn Murray influenced fellow Harvard psychologist David McClelland, who identified the three motive needs measured in this book's ALP model: achievement, affiliation, and power.

Jung was also cited by Maslow as one of the first psychologists to explore human potential as opposed to deficiency. Jung believed that the process of discovering our purpose, and living at our highest potential, could best be termed "individuation." In the procession of individuation, what he also called "self-realization," a person separates from the restraints of cultural and societal norms and steps into their highest potential. Jung believed this process required interaction with the collective shadow (i.e., society's adoption of its collective unacknowledged darker side). Maslow did not necessarily agree with this assessment, but it clearly influenced his thinking about the highest potential of human nature.

As noted earlier, Jung's concept of the shadow—the dark, unconscious aspects of our personality that reside within each of us—supports critical concepts in this book. Jung defined the shadow as our dark, rejected, instinctual side. It is also the side that we do our best to deny or repress. Impulses such as rage, lust, greed, and jealousy exist within the shadow, as do creativity, passion, and profound insight. The more open and honest you are about your own shadow, the greater your ability to integrate it into who you are and thus make your shadow a reservoir for positive aspects such as creativity and passion.

Jung (1927) also believed that the shadow exists at multiple levels. At the highest level is the collective shadow that holds all human memory at an unconscious level. You can think of it as the DNA (or building block) of our collective unconscious. Although the collective unconscious varies by culture and heritage, universal archetypes exist in the collective shadow, including familiar themes such as the heroic journey of an individual warrior. A contemporary example of this archetype is the character Luke Skywalker in the *Star Wars* movies, an example mirrored in many characters in classical Greek literature narratives.

Jung's concept of the *personal shadow* is closely aligned with the ideas of an equally famous psychiatrist, Sigmund Freud, and his notion of the id that represents our repressed unconscious impulses (i.e., illicit desires, basic human instincts, and selfishness). Despite our attempts to deny them, these base instincts exist just below the surface of our psyche. If you need proof, try pointing out an obvious shadow trait in someone you know and observe how quickly their denying, angry defenses go up. Jung said that enlightenment can happen only when we're willing to confront and embrace the darker shadow side of ourselves.

Our collective shadow has an enormous impact on all human behavior, and it's a topic that can be endlessly explored. However, this book focuses on how Jung's theories and writings can be applied to leadership behaviors, specifically how a leader's personal shadow can derail even the best leaders—especially during times of stress—resulting in destructive consequences.

Defining Leadership Shadows

Leadership shadows are defined in this book as the extreme, negative manifestations of our positive drivers. These shadows are based on irrational thoughts and unfounded fears that are maintained by limiting and masking our core beliefs. Table 3.1 is a graphic representation of how this book incorporates McClelland's three motive needs or drivers (achievement, affiliation, and power) and corresponding leadership styles (Achiever, Affirmer, and Asserter). The three leadership shadows, the dark or extreme side of the positive motive needs in the context of this book and the ALP framework, include Fear of Failure, Fear of Rejection, and Fear of Betrayal.

As noted previously, stress—that tense and taxing space we so often encounter in our professional and personal lives—is the trigger that engages our leadership shadow and often results in career (and relationship) limiting moves such as micromanaging, avoiding conflict, or refusing to trust others.

David McClelland: The Three Motive Need Drivers

Harvard psychologist David McClelland's book *Human Motivation* (1988), about the drivers of human motivation, is critical to the concepts that underpin the leadership framework presented here.

Table 3.1. McClelland's Three Drivers and Corresponding Actualized Leadership Styles

Motive Need	Leadership Style	Leadership Shadow
Achievement	Achiever	Fear of Failure
Affiliation	Affirmer	Fear of Rejection
Power	Asserter	Fear of Betrayal

In his book, McClelland identifies three motive needs that propel our behavior—Achievement, Affiliation, and Power—in a theory he calls the three-need or Acquired Need theory of human motivation. Here's how these motive needs shape the Achiever, Affirmer, and Asserter leadership profiles presented in this book's leadership model.

Achievers, those with a high need for achievement, are driven for success, improvement, and accomplishment. These leaders are primarily concerned with expertise and competence; they are detail-oriented, disciplined, focused, and well-organized. These individuals are also efficient, are rules-oriented, and prefer consistency and predictability. Under stress, however, their leadership shadow—Fear of Failure—is triggered and these same Achievers become narrow-minded, rigid micromanagers.

Affirmers, those with high affiliation needs, are warm and friendly. They focus more on interpersonal relationships and harmony, and less on results and outcomes. These leaders are primarily concerned with their connection to, and acceptance from, others; they are also loyal, trusting, and empathetic. When stress triggers their leadership shadow—Fear of Rejection—these individuals become overaccommodating, indecisive, and conflict-avoidant. As you might guess, this behavior often allows others to take advantage of these leaders.

Asserters, leaders with a high need for power, are candid, decisive, and courageous risk-takers. They are often viewed as natural leaders who challenge the status quo and drive results. Asserters are primarily concerned with control and are often skeptical and slow to trust others. When stress triggers their leadership shadow—Fear of Betrayal—these individuals become controlling, autocratic, and condescending, and they often manipulate or intimidate others to get their way.

Reading through the characteristics of Achievers, Affirmers, or Asserters, you're likely to immediately identify with one or more of the profiles. You should note this initial reaction to see how it tracks with the comprehensive ALP assessment included with this book.

Abraham Maslow: Self-Actualization

Maslow's work challenged the idea that satisfied, happy, and effective people were born that way and replaced it with the notion that anyone can achieve that status through internal growth and development as they move toward what he called "self-actualization." Self-actualization is the process of becoming or actualizing your highest self and realizing your highest potential. Maslow found that self-actualizing individuals connected deeply to a sense of purpose beyond the normal day-to-day and were grateful and humble. They often reported "peak experiences" during which they transcended the normal realms of possibility and understanding to gain a higher consciousness and engagement with their peak performance.

My research has focused on the role that self-actualization plays in leadership. Specifically, it serves as both a barometer of resiliency and a moderator of your leadership shadow. Simply put, the more self-actualized you are, the greater your ability to operate from a sense of abundance and strength, as opposed to scarcity and fear. Therefore, you become more resilient and are better able to manage the activation and intensity of your leadership shadow.

The inverse of this dynamic is true as well. If you are less self-actualized, then you'll experience the effects of your leadership shadow more frequently and with greater intensity (i.e., you'll be prone to micromanaging or will exhibit leadership behaviors rooted in scarcity and a sense of fear). Chapter 4 examines in greater detail the importance of self-actualization as the moderator of your leadership shadow.

Hierarchy of Needs

Maslow's most famous model, his Hierarchy of Needs, is a commonly accepted starting point for any discussion on human motivation (see Figure 3.1). According to Maslow's rankings (1954), four groups of basic, or deficiency, needs must be met before self-actualization can occur.

First, our physiological needs—food, water, sleep, and physical comfort—must be met. Next, we must feel safe and secure. Once these needs are met, we can focus on psychological needs including relationships, friends, feelings of self-esteem, and accomplishment. Finally, at the top of Maslow's pyramid are self-fulfillment needs and the achievement of our highest and most creative potential.

However, as Maslow illustrated, and as many later researchers have also pointed out, just because we satisfy one need does not necessarily mean that we automatically evolve to a higher order of behavior. Both research and everyday experience demonstrate that many individuals get stuck because of a deficiency at one level, which impedes their growth and development toward the ultimate goal of self-actualization.

Figure 3.1. Maslow's Hierarchy of Needs

Viktor Frankl: Personal Freedom and Paradoxical Intent

Austrian psychoanalyst Viktor Frankl has influenced an untold number of researchers, psychologists, and philosophers. He was one of the millions of people who experienced firsthand the horrific conditions and abuse of the Nazi concentration camps during World War II. It was a level of soul-crushing barbarism that destroyed the will of most; however, Frankl chose a unique response to the situation, and it was this response that gave him a sanity-saving (and ultimately life-saving) perspective that was the foundation of his best-selling book *Man's Search for Meaning*. Instead of focusing on the power of his tormentors, he focused on the only real power he had as the victim of the abuse: *the freedom to choose his response to the situation.*

Frankl's response to such hellish conditions is the basis of the first pillar of this book's model: we are free to choose our attitude and response to every situation (or person). Frankl's theory contains a powerful truth: when we react to others in fear and anger, we relinquish this freedom of choice. Ultimately, he realized that reclaiming this freedom gave him greater freedom than the prison guards who tormented him.

Stephen Covey echoed this sentiment in his famous book *The 7 Habits of Highly Effective People* (1990) when he coined the term "response-ability." Leaders who fail to take responsibility for their own actions and attitudes risk setting off a cascade of negative consequences for individual players, team members, departments, divisions, or even entire organizations.

Frankl also contributed a second powerful thematic driver for this book: the concept of paradoxical intent. Simply put, paradoxical intent is the concept that *the more we fear something, the more likely we are to experience it.* Frankl gives many examples in *Man's Search for Meaning*, both from his experiences in a concentration camp and from his private practice. A less somber example of paradoxical intent is insomnia. The more someone fears they'll never go to sleep, the less likely it is that sleep will come. Frankl instructed his sleepless patients to turn their attention toward staying awake as long as possible, thereby dispelling their fear of sleeplessness. Who hasn't worried so much about what might happen (e.g., failing an important test, being rejected by someone, or not falling asleep) that the thing we feared most (failure, rejection, or insomnia) is what ultimately happened?

Placed in this book's context, consider a high Achiever leader who operates at a low level of self-actualization. Even if the Achiever is well-organized, detailed-oriented, and efficient, any significant stress (for example, a lack of clear direction) will push this Achiever toward their "shadow" Achiever behaviors. In this case, the Achiever becomes rigid, narrow-minded, and worse, a classic micromanager. It is easy to see how this behavioral cycle will limit upward managerial mobility and ultimately fulfill paradoxical intent.

What's Next

Four theoretical frameworks were discussed in this chapter: Jung's legacy related to self-actualization, individual differences, and his concept of the shadow; McClelland's research into the three unique motive drivers that propel our behavior; Maslow's Hierarchy of Needs and the importance of self-actualization; and Frankl's liberating notion of reclaiming our freedom to choose our response and how to guard against experiencing paradoxical intent. The synthesis of these models and theories supports the comprehensive ALP framework that follows.

Chapter 4 steps away from the theoretical and moves directly to practical application. So, to fully take advantage of the content in the next chapter, make sure that you have completed the ALP online assessment at http://www.ALPFree.com. With the results of this assessment in hand, you'll be ready to explore in depth the three key leadership styles: Achiever, Affirmer, and Asserter. Importantly, you'll also learn more about the leadership shadows associated with each style and begin the process of meeting and integrating your shadow so that you can achieve your highest potential.

Chapter 4
Leader and Team Dynamics

What's in This Chapter?

» About the ALP Framework
» The Achiever Style
» The Affirmer Style
» The Asserter Style
» Integrating your Leadership Shadow with Cognitive Behavioral Therapy (CBT)
» The Actualized Performance Cycle
» What's Next

To confront a person with his own shadow
is to show him his own light.

—Carl Jung

This chapter is designed to give you a clear line of sight to your leadership shadow and an understanding of the fear that underlies it. It does not offer tips on time management or strategies for delegating more effectively since many other resources exist on these and other tactical strategies that make you a better leader. As such, this chapter is developmental and aimed at helping you consciously integrate your leadership shadow knowledge into how you work with others as a leader. The pathway to do this work is known as cognitive behavioral therapy (CBT).

CBT is a simple and very effective technique for objectively examining how our limiting thoughts and core beliefs trigger negative emotions, which in turn lead to suboptimal—if not outright dysfunctional—behaviors. This will be addressed in more depth later in this chapter.

The second section of this chapter introduces a framework for group culture and links leader style to team dynamics. In this section you will see how your style, or more specifically your leadership shadow, impacts those around you, especially your direct reports. Strong, micromanaging Achievers (as in the example above) create a *Detached* culture in which members check out both physically (e.g., leaving the office early) and psychologically (e.g., being distracted and disinterested in the task at hand). The tragic irony in this dynamic is that the more Achievers allow fear to drive their behavior, the more likely they are to experience the very thing they are trying hardest to avoid: failure. This is a perfect example of Frankl's notion of "paradoxical intent."

The Actualized Performance Cycle introduced at the end of this chapter is designed to help you better understand your style, both its strengths and limitations, your leadership shadow, and the culture you are likely to create and sustain. The well-researched, self-assessment part of the ALP is designed to provide greater insight into your style and the impact you have on others. This tool is unique in the marketplace in at least two significant ways.

First, the ALP is the only scientifically validated leadership assessment based on the work of Carl Jung that measures both our motive needs (including Maslow's notion of self-actualization) and our all-important leadership shadow (i.e., our leadership's dark side based on the work of Jung). Second, the ALP is the only assessment that links leadership effectiveness to well-researched group culture dynamics and measures how a leader's style and shadow impacts their direct reports and colleagues.

Note: Before beginning your work on this chapter, make sure you complete the free version of the ALP assessment available at http://www.ALPFree.com.

About the ALP Framework

The theoretical and philosophical underpinnings of the ALP Framework were noted in the opening sections of this book and examined in detail in Chapter 3. Now it's time to put these concepts to practical use in your professional life as a leader.

The ALP Framework includes three leadership styles—Achiever, Affirmer, and Asserter. Each style is a combination of dominant motive needs (or behavioral drivers) and your self-actualization score. To be clear, the term "Actualized Leader" indicates a leader high in self-actualization, irrespective of that individual's dominant motive or behavioral traits. The goal of the process is self-actualization growth that allows you to operate as an Actualized Achiever, Actualized Affirmer, or Actualized Asserter.

As such, your developmental goal is not to betray your innate tendencies. Rather, you should focus on growing your own self-actualization score rather than a higher score in a style you believe is more desirable. Doing so will play to your natural strengths and help you manage your own leadership shadow.

This chapter examines how leaders can achieve Actualized Leader status and reach their highest leadership potential. At the same time, doing this work will have an important tangential benefit of creating Dynamic cultures for your direct reports and colleagues. To take advantage of these benefits, you must closely examine your own leadership style and shadow in context of the three primary styles, Achiever, Affirmer, and Asserter. Summaries of these styles are listed below and graphically represented in the illustrations that follow (Figures 4.1–4.3).

THE ACHIEVER STYLE
Leadership Shadow: Fear of Failure

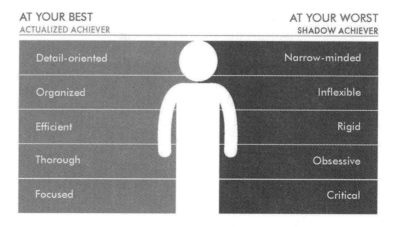

AT YOUR BEST ACTUALIZED ACHIEVER	AT YOUR WORST SHADOW ACHIEVER
Detail-oriented	Narrow-minded
Organized	Inflexible
Efficient	Rigid
Thorough	Obsessive
Focused	Critical

Figure 4.1. The Achiever Style

THE AFFIRMER STYLE
Leadership Shadow: Fear of Rejection

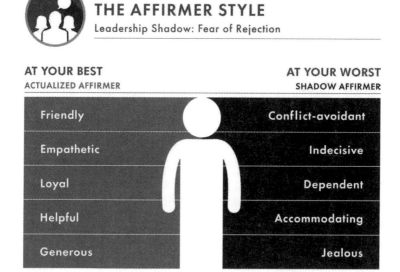

AT YOUR BEST ACTUALIZED AFFIRMER	AT YOUR WORST SHADOW AFFIRMER
Friendly	Conflict-avoidant
Empathetic	Indecisive
Loyal	Dependent
Helpful	Accommodating
Generous	Jealous

Figure 4.2. The Affirmer Style

THE ASSERTER STYLE
Leadership Shadow: Fear of Betrayal

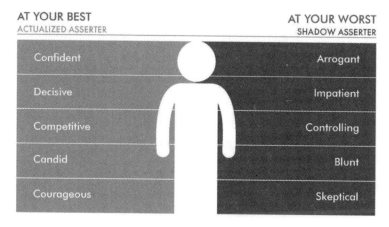

AT YOUR BEST ACTUALIZED ASSERTER		AT YOUR WORST SHADOW ASSERTER
Confident		Arrogant
Decisive		Impatient
Competitive		Controlling
Candid		Blunt
Courageous		Skeptical

Figure 4.3. The Asserter Style

Integrating Your Leadership Shadow with Cognitive Behavioral Therapy (CBT)

People are disturbed not by things, but by the views which they take of them.

—Epictetus (Greek Philosopher)

One reason the ALP Framework is so powerful is its direct connection to a well-known, evidence-based approach to understanding human behavior known as cognitive behavioral therapy (CBT). It is an approach that is widely used in a variety of clinical and non-clinical applications to improve performance and increase personal satisfaction and individual happiness. CBT is especially effective in treating anxiety and mood disorders. All three cycles of the leadership shadow, *Fear of Failure* (Achiever), *Fear of Rejection* (Affirmer), and *Fear of Betrayal* (Asserter), align with the methodologies associated with this CBT model.

To completely understand the importance of the CBT connection and the way it is used to analyze our behavioral patterns, here is a personal example taken from a very ordinary set of circumstances involving international travel with a colleague.

A few years ago, I was traveling back from France with a colleague. He and I had co-facilitated a well-received training event, and as a result he was relaxed and looking forward to reading a personal development book someone had recommended. I was not so relaxed and as a recovering Asserter with a high need for control (at the time), I was upset, worried, and anxious about getting home for a variety of personal and professional reasons.

Then, the all too familiar happened: an announcement that our flight had been delayed, followed by another one that the flight had been canceled. Of course, chaos ensued as we joined hundreds of other passengers charging the airline's customer service desk to reschedule their flights. While we waited in the predictably lengthy line to reschedule, my colleague seemed unconcerned and not at all put off by the delay or inconvenience.

He was calm and even jovial as he talked about how much he had enjoyed co-facilitating our event and how much he had learned. Of course, I was not a happy camper and spent the time worrying over my to-do list and all that wouldn't get done, even dwelling on the potential repercussions of not relieving my parents from taking care of my dog. As it turned out, all the sound and fury on my part was completely wasted energy since we easily caught another flight, and the delay and inconvenience were minimal.

I share this example to illustrate the wisdom in the quote from Epictetus. Clearly, my colleague had a more productive approach at the time. However, the story is a somewhat embarrassing episode of impatience on my part. It shows how two people can interpret the same situation differently and experience vastly different emotions. Behavioral and mental health professionals use the CBT framework to help their clients reframe events and setbacks, and to understand how their reactions impact relationships with colleagues, friends, and family members. This reframing helps build self-awareness and the ability to assess the rationality or validity of the approach we've taken. Once such awareness is achieved, CBT allows us to replace these irrational/incorrect thoughts with more rational/correct responses.

The CBT model also closely aligns with the widely recognized concept of emotional intelligence (EI or EQ), an area of study that has been exhaustively documented in books, seminars, and workshops. EI is important because it clearly shows the multiple intelligences that people possess, and in the context of this book this is what makes EI important to leadership effectiveness.

However, here is one caveat about the connection between CBT and EI. I believe behavior is triggered first by a thought, which subsequently triggers an emotional response that is either a less-than-optimal or outright-dysfunctional behavioral response. To truly develop your full potential as a leader (see Part IV for the Transformational Journey), the first step is to become aware of those thoughts so that you can "meet" them and ultimately integrate them into a full understanding of your own leadership shadow.

This thought to behavior dynamic is why the Leadership Shadow Cycle begins with the most common thoughts associated with each style before illustrating the emotions likely triggered by the thought and, finally, to the resulting behaviors. Understanding your thoughts and the limiting beliefs that trigger negative emotions is the only pathway to gaining control of your leadership shadow. Otherwise your emotions will control and manage you, which is not a viable leadership option.

With this bit of background as context and explanation, here is a deeper dive into some practical applications and how the Leadership Shadow Cycle impacts leadership effectiveness. This cycle includes the following:

» Fear of Failure
» Fear of Rejection
» Fear of Betrayal

The Dark Side of Achievement: Fear of Failure

Achievers desire perfection and have an underlying belief that their way is best. They often struggle with a sense of not feeling worthy and therefore focus on their accomplishments to prove their worth to the world and themselves. Unfortunately, the irrational thoughts that underlie the Fear of Failure Shadow trigger the emotions and behaviors that, over time, almost guarantee that Achievers will fail. Below is a summary of some of the thoughts, emotions, and behaviors that fuel this leadership shadow.

Table 4.1. The Fear of Failure Leadership Cycle

Irrational Thoughts	Unfounded Feelings	Self-defeating Behaviors
I have to always be perfect.	Inadequate	Becoming obsessive and nitpicky.
No one else can do this as well as I can.	Frustration	Being overly critical and micromanaging.
I am not enough without my accomplishments.	Shame	Taking on too many projects, or staying over-scheduled.

The Dark Side of Affiliation: Fear of Rejection

Affirmers desire connection to, and approval from, others. They have an underlying belief that relationships are paramount and separation or rejection from others must be avoided at all costs. They often struggle with not feeling wanted unless they are helping others. Unfortunately, the irrational thoughts that underlie the Fear of Rejection Shadow trigger the emotions and behaviors that, over time, guarantee they will experience the rejection and separation they are desperately trying to avoid. Below is a summary of some of the thoughts, emotions, and behaviors that fuel this leadership shadow.

Table 4.2. The Fear of Rejection Leadership Shadow Cycle

Irrational Thoughts	Unfounded Feelings	Self-defeating Behaviors
I cannot be alone.	Insecure	Staying in unhealthy relationships.
The needs of others are more important than my own.	Insignificant	Ignoring your own needs and being overly accommodating.
I should not anger others.	Weak	Allowing others to take advantage of you.

The Dark Side of Power: Fear of Betrayal

Asserters are natural leaders who crave power and like to be in control. They have an underlying belief that the world is not safe and that resources are scarce. They often have a very strong zero-sum mentality, meaning that if someone else wins then they, by default, lose because theirs is a world of scarcity, not abundance. They have difficulty trusting others and fear vulnerability, often waiting to be betrayed.

Unfortunately, the irrational thoughts that underlie the Fear of Betrayal Shadow trigger the emotions and behaviors that, over time, guarantee that they will experience the sense of betrayal and loss they are trying to avoid. Below is a summary of some of the thoughts, emotions, and behaviors that fuel this leadership shadow.

Table 4.3. The Fear of Betrayal Leadership Shadow Cycle

Irrational Thoughts	Unfounded Feelings	Self-defeating Behaviors
I have to always be in charge.	Control	Constantly maneuvering for more control and power.
People cannot be trusted.	Skeptical	Rarely putting your guard down or expressing vulnerability.
I am "right."	Arrogance	Being outspoken, autocratic, and sarcastic.

A Framework for Group Culture

Thus far we have focused specifically on you and your leadership style. The rest of this chapter examines the critical linkage between your leadership style and culture. As noted earlier, a leader's style and shadow impact the effectiveness and productivity of direct reports, but also may seriously damage teams, departments, and divisions within an organization. At the end of this chapter, the importance of this link will be clearly made when I introduce the Actualized Performance Cycle. But first, some more background.

The behavioral psychodynamics that underpin the leadership effectiveness approach taken in this book are based largely on the work of psychoanalyst Wilfred Bion, arguably the most influential group dynamics theorist. Here is a brief overview of Wilfred Bion's theory of group behavior and team dynamics, which makes explicit the connection between style and culture.

Bion, who served in the British army during the First World War and in the Royal Army Medical Corps as a psychiatrist during World War II, created the first cohesive framework for group development and performance that follows the psychodynamic tradition. Later in his career, Bion conducted pioneering research into human potential and group dynamics at The Tavistock Institute of Human Relations, a nonprofit established in 1947 and dedicated to applying psychoanalytic and open systems concepts to group and organizational life.

Bion (1961) professed that participation in group life is mandated by the nature of our existence as human beings and is absolutely essential "to lead a full life." He defined a group as three or more people who share the same mental set. Physical presence is not necessary to meet Bion's definition of a group—only a shared mental set. A shared mental set refers to a common link for the group members, such as a challenge, problem, activity, or shared memory.

Think of it this way: a group of strangers riding in an elevator, each getting off on different floors, shares a very close physical proximity but is not a group because there is no shared mental set. If the elevator gets stuck between floors, then a shared mental set—how do we escape?—emerges and the occupants become a group under Bion's definition.

The Two Modes of Group Behavior

It's important to appreciate that there are always two modes of group behavior operating simultaneously: (1) a conscious work group behavior; and (2) an unconscious basic assumption group behavior. The first work group behavior is the official, overt mode of behaviors focused on completing or solving the group's task or problem. This first group is grounded by reality and is therefore capable of containing the group's basic assumptions, fantasies, and anxiety about a situation or event. As you'll see in the Actualized Performance Cycle, the Dynamic dimension represents the work group aspect of group culture.

The second mode of group behavior includes behaviors that are based on the irrational fears and unconscious emotional needs of the group members. The manifestations of these fears and needs are known as Basic Assumption States (BAMS). There are three distinct types: Fight/Flight, Pairing, and Dependency. Each of these types creates a specific group culture (Detached, Dramatic, and Dependent); again, concepts I will address later in this chapter.

When acting under these BAMS, the group may act as if it is helpless, under attack, or in need of salvation. The work group and the basic assumption group operate simultaneously and it is this dynamic interplay between these two states that creates shared meanings and fantasies, and from which group culture emerges and is moderated by the overall Dynamic state of the work group.

The Three Elements of Group Culture

Bion's work illustrates two important distinctions about the multi-dimensional nature of group culture: the first distinction is that one level impacts the other; the second distinction is that culture is built upon basic assumptions. However, just because you understand the basic assumptions driving behaviors doesn't mean that this insight will ensure effectiveness. That's why it's important to understand where and how group culture is developed and reinforced.

For example, we often blame the leader for a dysfunctional group, but the leader's style is one of several factors that impacts culture. Group culture is complex, interrelated, and multifaceted. While many contextual aspects unique to each group do exist, our research suggests that group culture is created and sustained by three primary factors:

» Individual personalities of group members
» The context or "macro-environment" impacting the group
» Leader style

Individual Personalities of Group Members

While the overall culture and decision-making dynamics of a group ultimately determine its effectiveness, individual personalities do matter a great deal and can damage a team's overall culture.

Although research is limited, some studies do correlate the impact of personality on group dynamics and organizational success. For example, Howard and Howard (2000) and Judge, Higgins, Thoresen, and Barrick (1999) found that leaders who score higher in conscientiousness (the trait of being organized, focused, and efficient) gain greater levels of success. Group members with this trait are more likely to prepare for group meetings and are more focused on performance, regardless of leader personality (extroverted and outspoken, or introverted and more reserved). Note that conscientiousness is a trait often found in the Achiever style.

A second trait, agreeableness, is associated with being trusting, modest, empathetic, and collaborative. Individuals and group members scoring high in this trait are effective listeners, dependable, inclusive, and prefer to work together as a team to accomplish goals. However, this personality trait also tends to be conflict-avoidant and, at times, overly accommodating. This trait is most often found in the Affirmer style.

Finally, leaders who score high in need for stability may have issues related to anxiety, anger, willingness to be vulnerable, and impulsiveness. They are often moody, temperamental, and envious. However, these individuals can also be charming, charismatic, self-confident, and even bold and visionary. Not surprisingly, leaders with this trait tend toward lower levels of empathy and collaboration (Maccoby, 2000). Individuals and team members with this trait are likely to make favorable first impressions, but can become dissatisfied and disruptive if they perceive their effort is not fairly recognized. Both the positive and negative aspects of this trait are often found in the *Asserter* style.

The Context or Macroenvironment Impacting the Group
The second factor that impacts group culture is the context or big-picture challenges (macroenvironment, in academic speak) facing the group. For instance, is the business growing and expanding, or is it contracting? Are technology and the global environment driving innovation, or are they making the company's products and services obsolete? In addition to these big-picture factors, contemporary issues such as global competition, rapid advances in technology, and generational differences in the workplace impact group culture beyond the individual personality differences of group members.

Here is an example of how the macroenvironment can impact group culture. Consider a corporate board as our group and the impact that shareholder activism can have on board culture. Activist shareholders are more prevalent today than ever before and many want a direct line to the CEO and management team to express concerns, provide advice, and influence the activities of the organization. While this situation is undoubtedly more disruptive for the management team, it does impact the dynamics of the board and, as a result, the board culture.

As described in *The Director's Manual* (Browning and Sparks, 2016), activist shareholders may demand a seat on the board, which leads to a much deeper level of engagement, not only with the management team but also with the board itself. They often have goals that may be shorter-term in nature and perhaps inconsistent with the longer-term vision held by the board. In the worst case, this type of scenario can be very disruptive to the culture and dynamics of the board by severely damaging open, honest dialogue in the board room and creating tension among board members, resulting in a *Detached* board culture. In the best circumstances, however, over time the activist comes to better understand the organization's longer-term strategy and the existing board comes to understand the activist shareholder's views as well.

Impact of Leader Style on Culture

A leader with low self-actualization is more reactive, less resilient, and much more likely to manifest their leadership shadow when under stress, which adversely impacts the group's culture and performance. Again, the full range of how leader style affects culture is discussed later in the context of the Leadership Performance Cycle. For now, it is critical to understand that each leadership style creates and fosters a unique group culture.

As previously discussed, each of the four distinct leadership styles is associated with a dominant motive (behavioral) need of the leader:

» Achiever (achievement need)
» Affirmer (affiliation need)
» Asserter (power need)
» Actualized (self-actualization need; a moderator of the leadership shadows associated with the other three styles)

Three of these four leadership styles—Achiever, Affirmer, and Asserter—create less-than-optimal cultures and directly impact communication, problem solving, decision-making, and, ultimately, group member engagement. A more self-actualized leader, whether an Actualized Achiever, Actualized Affirmer, or Actualized Asserter, is more effective at creating and sustaining a Dynamic group culture.

The Detached Culture—Achiever Leadership Style
The sad irony is that Achievers, individuals who have a very high need for achievement, create a Detached, low-performing culture. Because of their need for absolute perfection, Achievers sweat every detail and micromanage their teams. This is a common dynamic in work group settings.

As a result, the culture created is grounded in emotions of anger and apathy, and detachment is the resulting impact on the group. Group members express anger either aggressively, with open conflict and personal attacks, or passively by disengaging psychologically or physically. Psychological disengagement manifests when the group becomes more interested in their mobile phones, iPads, or what's for lunch than in the purpose of the meeting.

Physical disengagement occurs when group members habitually arrive late, leave early, or miss meetings altogether. Whether the anger is expressed actively or passively, members in a *Detached* culture are not optimally positioned for candid discussions, healthy debate, and rational decision-making.

Characteristics of the Detached Group Culture
 » **Patterns of Behavior:** Disagreement, dissent, open conflict, and tardiness.
 » **Norms:** Members are distracted and disengaged, members and the leader should be challenged.
 » **Values:** People are lazy and need to be carefully supervised and managed; anger and apathy.

» **Basic Assumptions:** There is an enemy, either from within or outside the group, which must be fought.

The Dramatic Culture—Affirmer Leadership Style

The Dramatic culture is created and sustained by Affirmer leaders who are primarily motivated by a need for affiliation, and are focused on maintaining warm, harmonious interpersonal relationships. To contrast this culture to that of the Achiever, imagine the extreme end of the spectrum from the Detached culture. Replace anger with kindness, rudeness with politeness, and despair with hope. While this group culture might sound more appealing, the result is the same degree of poor decision-making and group member disengagement.

These leaders need to be accepted and approved by the group at all costs. To this end, the group norm is one of politeness and friendliness to the extreme. Difficult or uncomfortable discussions are avoided or tabled for offline conversations that rarely occur. Although warm and personally supportive, the Dramatic culture lacks collegial candor and frankness. Members often self-censor to avoid breaking the group norm of politeness and agreement.

This culture is grounded in unrealistic hope for the future, which often spirals down to frustration and despair. Because candor and conflict are often avoided, group members often leave meetings feeling frustrated and exasperated with the lack of progress or action.

Characteristics of the Dramatic Group Culture
» **Patterns of Behavior:** Warm, friendly, and very social; problems are swept under the rug.
» **Norms:** Politeness, empathy, and accommodating the social needs of group members.
» **Values:** Trusting and hope for a better future, but frustration that can lead to despair is beneath the surface of warmth due to poorly optimized productivity or the enforcement of equitable performance standards.

» **Basic Assumptions:** Relationships with others are paramount and expectations for a brighter future will soon be realized.

The Dependent Culture—Asserter Leadership Style

It stands to reason that most business leaders have a great need for power and thus exhibit the Asserter leadership style. The resulting *Dependent* culture is grounded in fear and anxiety and exists only with the collusion of a leader that encourages dependency. Whether in *Fortune* 500 companies or nonprofit organizations, research has shown that this Asserter leadership style is the most common culture in Corporate America (Harvey, 1988; Sparks, 2002).

Characteristics of the Dependent Group Culture

» **Patterns of Behavior:** Compliance, appeals to the leader for direction, lack of accountability.
» **Norms:** The leader knows best, play it safe and don't take risks, and don't ever disagree with the leader (especially in public).
» **Values:** Obedience to the leader, reliance on his or her direction, asking for help is expected.
» **Basic Assumptions:** The group lacks sufficient maturity and expertise to operate without the ongoing support and guidance of the leader.

The Dynamic Culture—Actualized Leadership Style

Group members are realistic, engaged, passionate, and collaborative. This culture is not without some conflict as members care deeply about their roles and purpose, but conflict is openly discussed and managed effectively. There is a collegial candor atmosphere where people speak their minds openly and respectfully, and group members are encouraged to take risks, challenge the status quo, and support each other.

Characteristics of the Dynamic Group Culture

» **Patterns of Behavior:** High levels of engagement, collegial candor, and passion.

» **Norms:** Members trust each other, mutual accountability, creativity, and innovation.

» **Values:** People are basically trustworthy and do not need to be managed.

» **Basic Assumptions:** People can be trusted and we live in a world of abundance.

The Actualized Performance Cycle

When leader style/shadow and culture are linked together, the Actualized Performance Cycle is complete. Figure 4.4 is a graphic illustration of the dynamic interplay between leader style and group culture.

As you will note, the leader style is listed from *high* level of directive activity to *low*. Achievers have the highest level of directive activity and focus on the task at hand. Their tendency to micromanage and stay involved with the details creates the lowest-performing group culture, Detached.

Affirmers follow next, with a high level of directive activity, but in this instance, it is usually focused more on the interpersonal dynamics and human relations of the group. They tend to create Dramatic cultures, lower-performing cultures that often lack candor where obvious problems are either ignored or swept under the rug.

The Asserter represents a moderate degree of directive activity, focused on both the task and interpersonal relationships, but does not usually get into the details. Even though they often create a Dependent culture where members may be afraid to take a risk or offer a competing perspective, this work climate tends to perform at higher levels than either Detached or Dramatic.

Finally, the Actualized approach, whether Actualized Achiever, Actualized Affirmer, or Actualized Asserter, has the lowest level of directive activity and is more effective at creating the space and runway necessary for a group to grow and develop.

HIGH   **Level of Directive Activity**   LOW

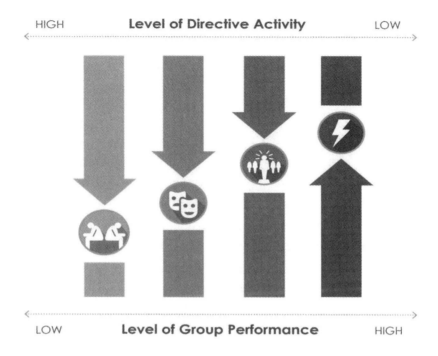

LOW   **Level of Group Performance**   HIGH

Figure 4.4. The Actualized Performance Cycle

In this instance, the leader focuses on three tasks:

» Providing a strategic direction for the group.
» Providing the necessary resources and occasional air cover necessary to support and shield the group from other organizational dysfunction.
» Staying out of the way.

My experience in twenty-five years of organizational consulting tells me that the third element—staying out of the way—although difficult, is the most effective strategy for leaders to adopt in the long term. Therefore, irrespective of your style, the common goal should be to grow and develop your self-actualization so that you become more self-aware, less reactive, and better able to resist the primal tendencies that emerge under stress and tempt us to indulge our leadership shadow.

What's Next

This chapter presented a detailed discussion on both leader style and group culture, and closed with the introduction of the Actualized Performance Cycle. As noted, the goal for each leader is to develop our self-actualization so that we get out of our own way and realize our fullest potential and highest purpose. Part Three of the book, starting with Chapter 5, will operationalize self-actualization and leadership by examining the characteristics or attributes that Actualized Leaders display.

There are nine attributes that have statistically significant correlations with self-actualization, and they are categorized in three domains: Cognition (how Actualized Leaders think), Emotion (how Actualized Leaders feel), and Behavior (what Actualized Leaders do). Chapter 5 introduces the three attributes associated with Cognition: objectivity, hyperfocus, and optimal time orientation (OTO). Leader interviews are provided for each attribute.

Part III
Actualized Leadership

Chapter 5

Cognition:
How Actualized Leaders Think

What's in This Chapter?

» Introduction: The 9 Attributes of Actualized Leaders
» Objectivity: John Allison
» Hyperfocus: Fred Whitfield
» Optimal Time Orientation (OTO): Jeff Brown
» What's Next

Introduction

The 9 Attributes of Actualized Leaders represent three specific modes of being—thinking, feeling, and doing—that self-actualized individuals engage in more frequently. These nine characteristics have been identified and validated by years of research which correlates different characteristics with higher self-actualization scores. In the final analysis, enhancing and developing these nine characteristics will help you become more self-actualized and reach your highest potential.

The 9 Attributes of Actualized Leaders occur in three domains: Cognition, Emotion, and Behavior. Although there is some overlap, for the most part there are three attributes for each domain. This chapter examines the three attributes related to cognition and how Actualized Leaders think.

As you read this section, it is important to relate these three modes of being back to the section on Cognitive Behavioral Therapy (CBT) as a method for personal development and growth. Unlike other schools of thought that focus on only one element of our being (e.g., Behaviorism), CBT considers all three (Cognition, Emotion, and Behavior) and their connection to our development.

As previously discussed, CBT begins with understanding how our thoughts impact our mood and overall disposition by triggering different emotions. Thinking negative thoughts, having a scarcity mindset (as opposed to an abundance mindset), and assuming worst-case scenarios create a whole series of negative emotions. Once negative emotions, such as anger, fear, or jealousy, are activated, they often trigger less than optimal behaviors that may be outright dysfunctional.

When we apply CBT to Actualized Leadership, we can understand our Thinking/Feeling/Doing Shadow Cycle. This process allows us to objectively and rationally step back from a situation and consider the validity of our thoughts, emotions, and behaviors. In this manner, we gain (or regain) control of our thoughts and emotions, allowing us to respond with thoughtful intention instead of reacting (or overreacting) with emotion.

In my many years of research and consulting, I have never encountered a leader who scored high in all nine attributes. You should think of your score on the 9 Attributes of Actualized Leaders as an opportunity and consider the feedback as insight into specific areas on which to focus for improvement. Appendix B provides a list of developmental resources for every aspect of the ALP, including the nine attributes.

The rest of this chapter examines the three cognitive attributes of Actualized Leaders: objectivity, hyperfocus, and optimal time orientation (OTO).

Please note: If you would like to complete the full version of the ALP in order to receive your scores on your entire motive need profile, leadership shadow frequency and intensity activation, and the 9 Attributes of Actualized Leaders, please visit http://www. ActualizedLeadership.com/ALP.

Attribute #1: Objectivity

Dispassionate objectivity is itself a passion, for the real and for the truth.
—Abraham Maslow

You can twist perception, reality won't budge.
—"Show Don't Tell," Rush

Introduction

Psychologist Abraham Maslow often began discussions about the characteristics of self-actualizing individuals with what is likely the most important attribute—the need to be objective. According to Maslow, these individuals are blessed with "a more efficient perception of reality and more comfortable relations with it" (1987). As such, self-actualized people have an enhanced ability to "detect the spurious, the fake, and the dishonest in personality . . . [and] to judge correctly and efficiently" (1987). So, given its importance, what exactly does being objective mean in the context of this book?

Being objective does not mean that an individual is tough-minded without any emotion or intuition. According to researcher Gayle Privette (2001), this state of perception is easily viewed as just another form of bias. As discussed in this book, our leadership shadow filters our experiences and skews the data we observe. Thus, objectivity does not come to us easily or naturally. As leaders, it's a perception/reality conundrum that can be solved only through active management of our own leadership shadow and by having the courage and energy to develop the required self-awareness to confront the true facts of a situation regardless of our own "wishes, hopes, fears, [and] anxieties."

Leaders must also look beyond any biases that are built either on their own "theories and beliefs" or those of their own cultural group. When we are objective, we are better positioned to accurately critique or judge a situation and make decisions based on the actual facts, allowing us to face reality and our circumstances.

OBJECTIVITY

Accurately and efficiently discerning the facts of a given situation without being influenced by personal feelings or sentiment, or by external opinions or expectations.

Why This Attribute Is Important for Self-Actualization and Leadership

Ancient philosophers and modern-day writers, from Aristotle to Jim Collins (author of *Good to Great*) and Stephen Covey (the late author of *The 7 Habits of Highly Effective People*), all affirm the existence of an external, objective reality. The challenge for leaders is to act in accordance with this "natural law" and to develop the ability to "confront the brutal facts" of our situation, as Jim Collins (2001) points out. Once we make this leap of faith, the best decisions are usually self-evident. Here are three key reasons why being objective is critical to a leader's self-actualization quest.

First, practicing objectivity allows us to be "cognitively correct" (Maslow's way of saying face the facts). Such cognitive correctness encourages more openness to experience and less rigidity. Second, being objective builds our capacity to lead others since it forces a greater focus on problem solving rather than egocentric solutions that tap into our leadership shadows or the personalities at play in a situation. Finally, being objective is required to experience the dividend of self-actualization: flow. In order to achieve flow, Privette (2001) found that individuals must have a "clear focus" on the task at hand. She defines clear focus as "seeing what is there without [the] obstruction that comes from emotional and cognitive biases."

However, being objective does not give any leader, or nonleader for that matter, a direct line of sight into reality. We are all human and fallible, and our own experiences and emotions often cloud our perception and judgment. In *The 7 Habits of Highly Effective People*, Covey (1990) states that our mental maps (perception) are never the actual territory (reality). Therefore, changing our perception does not affect the reality. In fact, these changes move us further away from our self-actualized destination and potential.

• • • • •
ATTRIBUTE IN ACTION: JOHN ALLISON

John Allison is the retired chief executive officer of BB&T Bank and president and chief executive officer of the Cato Institute. He currently serves as a director with Moelis & Company and as an executive in residence at Wake Forest University.

What is, is. We may not like it but reality is irrefutable; it is what it is. Successful individuals (and successful businesses) must engage in reality, make decisions, and take actions based on the facts of their situations.

Francis Bacon famously said that "nature to be mastered, must first be obeyed." The law of gravity is a fundamental reality, but that does not mean we cannot engineer and build airplanes to fly. They simply must be constructed within the law of gravity as opposed to denying it.

There are three major mistakes in thinking—epistemological errors—that can and do have a serious negative impact on your life and the lives of others. The first error is the sin of psychological evasion. When we avoid examining data or information that threatens our deeply held beliefs, we detach from reality. And when this occurs, we aren't just missing a data point; we are actively avoiding it. In my view, this is a cardinal sin—both in business and in life—and leads to a psychologically dangerous and unhealthy place.

The second mistake is the belief that popularity equates to validity. Reality exists independent of popularity. Subprime lending was very popular, but it was also very destructive. Galileo's notion that the earth revolved around the sun was not very popular, but his assertion's lack of popularity didn't change the fact that it was true.

Finally, reality exists independent of authority. Just because a person in power states that something is true does not make it so. Authority-based assertions, which often exist as the enemy of reason, challenge us to engage reality and make decisions based on the facts of a situation rather than our preferences, popularity, or authority.

• • • • •

Attribute #2: Hyperfocus

Concentration is the secret of strength.
—Ralph Waldo Emerson

If you chase two rabbits, both will escape.
—Unknown

Introduction

Hyperfocus is the attribute that lays the foundation for the *Peak Performance Sequence* of Actualized Leaders. It's the ability to be laser-focused on the task at hand and unaffected by external distractions, such as email, telephone calls, and text messages. It is a baseline requirement that allows us to engage in peak behaviors and trust ourselves and our teammates in the peak performance process.

| HYPERFOCUS

An intense form of mental concentration or visualization focused on a task or activity.

Why This Attribute Is Important for Self-Actualization and Leadership

Hyperfocus is required for leading effectively because it is the mental state necessary to totally immerse oneself in the task at hand. In his book *Deep Work*, Cal Newport (2016) states that professional activities performed in distraction-free environments not only enhance your cognitive abilities and improve your skills but also produce optimal, more elite-level results. Hyperfocus is characterized by two manifestations: *concentration* and *visualization.*

Concentration is what we typically think of as a direct focus on or total immersion in the task at hand. Many musicians, artists, and athletes often report this kind of intense attention when segments of time, sometimes entire days, are lost to their activity.

Visualization is the concept of imagining a successful outcome ahead of the task or activity. Athletes such as basketball and football players often use this technique when they imagine success from the free throw line or before attempting a field goal. Other famous sports and entertainment celebrities including Oprah Winfrey, Jim Carrey, Jack Nicklaus, and Tiger Woods credit visualizing the desired outcome for their extraordinary success.

The world-famous guru of emotional intelligence Daniel Goleman (2015) gives a compelling business case for why leaders today need to *pay attention* to their *attention*. In his best-selling book *Focus: The Hidden Driver of Excellence*, he makes the case that the best way for leaders to raise the level of energy and attention in their organizations is to first pay attention to their own level of focus. Goleman notes that attention and focus are like muscles—the more you use them, the more developed they become. On the other hand, if you go through life distracted and inattentive, these same attention "muscles" will wither and atrophy.

Why is attaining this state of hyperfocus such a challenge? First, we live in a society that reinforces distraction. We participate in conference calls in the airport or on the way to the grocery store, and we multitask and self-medicate our way through life. Second, we are hyperconnected to every aspect of our lives—writing or reading important memos while emailing or texting with our children, colleagues, and friends—which keeps us from true focus on any single aspect of our lives or responsibilities. Such skimming across the surface of our lives makes it possible to never commit to anything fully, always leaving open the option for something better to come along. We can and do miss the opportunities available to us by "chasing two rabbits," and, sadly, they both often elude us.

Here's a suggestion—the next time you're feeling distracted, consciously remove the distraction and give yourself permission to be lost in the moment. You can do this at work or at the dinner table, even when you're staring down a perfect meal that is calling out to be shared with your Facebook friends. Instead, focus on the delicious meal in front of you and savor it along with the company and conversation that surround it. Your dinner companion, restaurant neighbors, and Facebook friends will appreciate it more than you know—and so will you.

• • • • •
ATTRIBUTE IN ACTION: FRED WHITFIELD

Fred Whitfield is the president and vice chairman of the Charlotte Hornets.

I've been blessed to have been involved in collegiate and professional sports for most of my career. From playing and coaching to operating and managing a professional sports team, I am a firm believer that total concentration and focus is absolutely essential to achieve success at an elite level. During my time as a collegiate player, and in graduate school completing law and business degrees, I learned that sustained concentration is the key for personal effectiveness. Moreover, it's not just concentration during a game or taking an exam that's important. While critical for success, we must also have total focus and dedication during our times of practice or study to develop the necessary skills and obtain the relevant knowledge to help us perform better than our opponent. In sports, every second counts. It is not uncommon to break down a film and realize that a key but often understated moment in a game, whether a foul or turnover, can be the turning point and the difference between winning and losing. Leaders, just like elite players, cannot afford to let their concentration slip.

My personal philosophy is that in order to truly be successful in any endeavor, you owe it to yourself and your teammates to create a bold and inspiring vision for the future. I don't believe that mediocrity or incremental improvement inspires greatness. Nor are either of these deserving of our total concentration and focus. It is only when leaders create a bold and audacious goal for a future state that the energy and focus necessary for true greatness can be created and sustained. I've never seen a business, sports team, or player thrive without a strong goal. When you have the courage to dream big, and the discipline to focus on achieving your objective, you will live and lead at your highest potential.

• • • • •

Attribute #3: Optimal Time Orientation (OTO)

Whatever the present moment contains, accept it as if you had chosen it. This will miraculously transform your whole life.
—Eckhart Tolle

Surrender to what is. Let go of what was. Have faith in what will be.
—Sonia Ricotti

Introduction
Optimal Time Orientation (OTO) is the notion of living primarily in the present moment. OTO is a necessary mental state for many optimal behaviors, including the three behaviors of Actualized Leaders: candor, flow, and solitude. OTO is sometimes characterized as having a "balanced time perspective" toward the three arenas of time: past, present, and future. Individuals with a balanced time perspective and who maintain an OTO are psychologically more focused and optimistic, as well as physically healthier and more resilient.

OTO

A balanced sense of time where the individual lives primarily in the present moment.

Why This Attribute Is Important for Self-Actualization and Leadership
Leaders who practice OTO live and work primarily in the present moment. However, they occasionally refer to the past with a sense of satisfaction or look to the future with a positive expectation. Actualized Leaders with OTO can reflect on the past without succumbing to a sense of guilt or regret because such reflection is done with a "lessons learned" mindset. They can likewise look ahead without becoming paralyzed by fear and anxiety because they

have a mindset that such activity is essential to making strategic, sustainable decisions. However, it's important to note that a leader with OTO will spend most of their focus and energy on the present moment.

In many ways, OTO leaders are mindful leaders. A simple definition of this contemporary cultural notion is "paying attention on purpose without judgment." Mindful individuals are better able to manage stress, are more resilient, and even sleep better. Moreover, mindfulness enhances enjoyment of a range of sensual pleasures, from savoring food and wine to listening to music more intensely.

As noted earlier, the many distractions in our lives stand in the way of being mindful. Yes, allowing our minds to wander is very human and can lead to creative and innovative solutions, but it is important to balance such toggling between the past, present, and future. Too much rumination on the past can sap mental energy by dredging up feelings of guilt and resentment about past decisions or circumstances. And if we spend our mental energy focused on what may happen in the future, we are likely to experience fear and anxiety. Either way, we rob ourselves of the only self-actualizing moment that matters—the present one.

If you want to develop your own OTO, here are some activities to consider:

- » Take time every day for a fifteen-minute walk.
- » Meditate for five minutes every morning.
- » Make simple, stress-reducing breathing exercises a daily habit.
- » Become a *unitasker* by focusing completely on one task at a time. Reward yourself with multiple short breaks.
- » Practice daily moments of mindfulness. Purposely pay attention to routine moments in your life, from sunrises to your children interacting at home.

Eckhart Tolle reminds us that most stress is caused by "being here, but wanting to be there." Embrace your "here," wherever that may be, because when you do, you free yourself to find meaning and purpose in your current circumstances.

• • • • •
ATTRIBUTE IN ACTION: JEFFREY J. BROWN

Jeff Brown (JB) is the chief executive officer of Ally Financial Inc.

In my experience, allowing yourself to live and work in the moment is crucial to performing at your highest level. Reflecting on the past and planning for the future are critical orientations to maintain, but they should not exist at the expense of living in the present.

In order to effectively embrace a healthy sense of OTO, I think it's essential to allow yourself and your teammates to make mistakes. Working in the present moment allows you to execute well on the operational side of the house. And when you combine that with an understanding and acceptance that mistakes will occur (and that those mistakes make learning available), you release yourself and others to perform at the highest level.

I do think that leaders must attend to all three of the time-orientation arenas. I often find that when I do look back and reflect on the past, I am reminded of what we've accomplished and how far we've come. Likewise, looking to the future for strategic development provides the necessary vision to inspire myself and my teammates to grow and succeed. Having said that, I am a very strong believer in focusing on the current reality first. Maybe I'm too practical, but I think that it's tempting to drift toward a "wouldn't it be nice" future state at the expense of ignoring—or even denying—the current reality. Leaders must be able to maintain a critical sense of balance between focusing on the current situation and creating a strategic vision for the future.

A not-so-obvious irony related to OTO is that in order to optimize this mental attribute, you must attend to your physical health and well-being on a routine basis. Exercising, particularly running, every day early in the morning provides the solitude and space for me to both reduce stress and think about and prepare for the day ahead. When I follow a routine of physical exercise, the ability to live and work in the present moment with an OTO becomes easier, and I am more effective.

• • • • •

What's Next

This chapter began with a discussion of the link between the 9 Attributes of Actualized Leaders and CBT and their connection to identifying and breaking the Thinking/Feeling/Doing Leadership Shadow Cycle. Following that introduction, the three attributes associated with cognition were discussed. Chapter 6 will explore the three attributes associated with emotion and how Actualized Leaders feel. These attributes are courage, trust, and self-acceptance, and interviews from leaders discussing the relative importance of these attributes to living and leading at your highest potential are included in the chapter.

Chapter 6

Emotion:

How Actualized Leaders Feel

What's in This Chapter?

Introduction

Emotions are a critical part of who we are and therefore are connected to how we lead. It is often said that to accomplish anything great, passion must be ever-present. Emotional intelligence (EI or EQ) and the critical role it plays in leader behavior (Goleman, 1995; 2002) have been increasingly recognized over the past twenty years. Negative emotions such as anger, jealousy, or fear drive negative behaviors that often derail an individual's career progression. The Leadership Shadow Cycle allows you to gain an understanding of some of the more common thoughts that trigger these counterproductive emotions, an understanding that will ultimately allow you to take charge and manage these emotions rather than let these emotions manage you.

Self-actualization and leadership research has identified three approximate emotional states that profoundly impact achievement of your highest potential and your effectiveness in working with and leading others. These three emotions are courage, trust, and self-acceptance. They are discussed in this chapter, and each is complemented with an interview of an accomplished leader who provides a practical, applied perspective on its importance to your success.

Attribute #4: Courage

Courage is not simply one of the virtues, but the form of every virtue at the testing point.

—C. S. Lewis

Life shrinks or expands in proportion to one's courage.

—Anais Nin

Introduction

Nelson Mandela famously said, "Courage is not the absence of fear, but the triumph over it." Framed in this context, courage is a powerful incentive to rise above our normal selves and reach our highest potential. Courage is the attribute that helps us overcome self-defeating, limiting behaviors and fears lurking in our leadership shadows and bridge the gap between our current state and our desired highest potential state.

COURAGE

The mental or moral strength to venture, persevere, and withstand danger, fear, or difficulty.

Why This Attribute Is Important for Self-Actualization and Leadership

"Courage" comes from the Latin word *cor*, which means to tell the story of who we are with "all of your heart." Courage, as Mandela says, is not fearlessness, nor is it bravado or reckless abandon. Rather, courage is about managing fear so that you can step into vulnerability with confidence.

In his book *The Gift of Fear*, Gavin de Becker (1995) explains how fear, manifested in our fight/flight response, is essential to our survival. This ancient survival instinct is programmed to emerge and warn us of danger, regardless of whether the threat is potential violence at the end of a dark, deserted alley or the inevitable arc of a destructive relationship.

EnPro Industries uses a powerful exercise (called *myVoice*) that helps its leadership program participants experience courage with their whole heart. Using a structured process, participants are instructed to consider an event or experience from the past that has affected their lives. After answering a series of questions aimed at drawing out the details of the experience, they are given time to prepare their story. Participants are then invited to share their story with the entire group. The experience is always a powerful, emotional, and slightly intimidating experience. However, it is a true catalyst for personal growth and transformation.

Courage is the testing point that carries us through vulnerability and connects us to our highest potential. It strengthens our better selves so that rather than reacting to our fears by micromanaging (Fear of Failure), avoiding conflict (Fear of Rejection), or intimidating others (Fear of Betrayal), we are able to acknowledge and rise above them. For Achievers, it is about stepping into ambiguity and finally letting go of perfection. For Affirmers, it is about stepping into confrontation and letting go of the need for approval. And for Asserters, it is about stepping into vulnerability and letting go of the myth of control.

Jung said that we are not the sum of the things that have happened to us; rather, we are who we choose to become. The myVoice exercise helps you understand what has shaped you up to this point and to calculate the price you may be paying for keeping those core beliefs. Often, you realize that you must let the past go so that you can claim your future. Courage is the testing point and the only path to reclaim this inherent freedom to chart your own course. Is your current path shrinking or expanding?

• • • • •
ATTRIBUTE IN ACTION: THE MOST REVEREND MICHAEL B. CURRY

Michael B. Curry is the presiding bishop and primate of The Episcopal Church.

"Be not afraid!" We live in a dangerous world where our instinct—our fight/flight response—can, and often does, take hold. Many of the fears that we face in the world today are very real, and I share that fear with others. And yet, God commands us to "be not afraid." It is through faith, meditation, prayer, and solitude that we can reconnect with our courage to act faithfully.

A challenge for many of us is to integrate courage with humility. The Latin root word for humility is *humus*, which means dirt. This word serves to remind us that we are from dirt, and "unto dirt we shall return." This is an important reminder for us all to establish and maintain an authentic sense of connection to others. Humility does not mean that you are timid or lacking confidence. Timothy 1:7 reminds us that we were not created with a spirit of timidity, but rather with courage and self-control.

I believe that humility actually makes it easier to be courageous. When we're humble we are less concerned about what others think of us, or about trying to be perfect. This state liberates us to act with decisive and courageous action. In my mind, courage and humility go hand in hand, especially when we remember the wise words of C. S. Lewis: "humility isn't thinking less of your-self, rather, it's thinking of yourself less often."

Now, there is a nuance here that one has to carefully moni-tor, and that is the state of false humility. False humility is just a deceptive and manipulative way to be proud and vain, and is just as destructive as pride and arrogance. So one must reflect on our origin and what we shall return to during times of solitude and prayerful meditation. Our faith calls us to be courageous and to temper our courageous acts with faith and humility.

• • • • •

Attribute #5: Trust

The best way to find out if you can trust somebody is to trust them.
—Ernest Hemingway

Few things help an individual more than to place responsi-bility upon him, and to let him know that you trust him.
—Booker T. Washington

Introduction

Trust is the currency of leadership; without it, optimal performance, creativity, and innovation in the workplace are not possible. To be clear, in the context of this book the word "trust" refers principally to your willingness as a leader to extend trust to others. I am not using "trust" in the sense of being trustworthy, which has more to do with leadership characteristics, such as authenticity and integrity.

Trust is a foundational requirement for other key self-actualization elements to exist, including vulnerability and forgiveness. Unfortunately, trust is in short supply in our society, even though we know that a full, daring, and "wholehearted life" (to quote Brené

Brown) is not possible without trust. Instead, we live our lives in a trust-but-verify mode, scanning, watching, and waiting to be betrayed. Whether it's asking direct reports for constant updates or reviewing the browser history of our partner, a lack of trust prevents us from having the career or life we want.

TRUST

A confident expectation of something; a reliance on the integrity and ability of another.

Why This Attribute Is Important for Self-Actualization and Leadership

Trust is the most precious gift we give to another person, and once it is destroyed, it is very difficult to reestablish. Yes, it can be rebuilt, but the analogy of a crumpled piece of paper is perhaps most helpful: you can straighten the sheet back out over time, but even when it's flat, it's never quite the same.

But there is another level of trust that is critical for self-actualization: trusting yourself. In fact, Maslow points out that all his self-actualizing subjects shared a common characteristic: they trusted their judgment, gut, and instinct and did not seek validation from others. In short, Maslow's subjects had their own internal validation barometer. Where does your barometer currently reside? Do you trust yourself, or do you seek approval and validation from others? These questions are particularly germane to Affirmers!

So, what does all of this mean for leadership? Recently, a group of executives was asked to list the three people they trusted the most. After parents, they typically mentioned siblings and spouses, with an occasional best friend. In this exercise, no one named their boss. However, when this same group was asked to list the three people who had the greatest impact on their happiness, "boss" was listed in every instance.

If you were to participate in this exercise, you may be tempted to refer to your boss in agreement, but I would encourage you, as a leader, to think about your coworkers and direct reports. How would they answer that question? Do you trust them, their ability, their work ethic, and their capability? Or, do you practice a trust-but-verify approach with them? You have a tremendous responsibility for their happiness—are they satisfied or parched?

Asserters with a high need for power and control are most challenged by the topic of trust (at least in relation to the Actualized Leader framework). The late Harvard psychologist David McClelland referred to these individuals as the engineers who build our skyscrapers and the generals who fight our wars. But despite the positive aspects of this penchant for action in Asserters, such unwillingness to extend trust, experience vulnerability, or grant forgiveness creates an illusion of security that can easily become a cage. Once trapped inside, it is difficult to escape the confines and genuinely connect with others on an authentic level.

If you are an Asserter, you might be thinking that trust leads only to betrayal. Yes, betrayal is always a possibility, but risk is a part of what it means to be human and to live a wholehearted life. Retired Bank of America Chairman and CEO Hugh McColl told me that he made a conscious decision to trust others during his time leading Bank of America. He said he continued to extend trust even when he was betrayed.

When I asked him why, he said that working in an environment without trust would have been limiting and ultimately unfulfilling. When I pointed out that he still could have built the bank and been successful without this attribute, he agreed in principle that such an outcome might have been possible, but added, "what would have been the point?" Take a moment to reflect on that insight, and act to extend trust to someone who deserves a chance in your life. You will either gain a friend or learn a lesson for life, as Hemingway pointed out, and either way, you will be richer for trying.

• • • • •
ATTRIBUTE IN ACTION: HUGH L. MCCOLL, JR.

**Hugh McColl is the retired chairman and chief
executive officer of Bank of America.**

If you want to be an effective leader, you must trust your team-mates. Trust is not a nice-to-have quality; it is an absolute must. Trust is the foundation of the social contract that we all enter into when we work with others in any setting. It's the "white space" between the boxes and titles on the organizational chart that ulti-mately determines success.

I trusted everyone at kickoff. When I look back at my career, one thing that I am very proud of is that no one ever had to earn my trust. I trusted others implicitly and always maintained a con-fident expectation in their motivation, attitude, and effort. Now, having said that, there were those over the years who lost my trust. Once my trust had been violated, there was no going back for that individual.

Let me talk about what trust is, and why it's so important for leaders. First, trust cannot be faked. It must come from a genuine and authentic concern for others and their well-being. In other words, you have to actually care about your teammates. As I said earlier, it is the foundation of every social contract in our lives. I learned in the United States Marine Corps that leaders lead from the front, and the troops eat first. In other words, take care of those around you before you take care of yourself. Trust is established and communicated by what you do, not by what you say. Over my career I never asked anyone to do something that I either hadn't done or wasn't currently doing, and that's a key part of building trust.

From a leadership perspective, it is so important because one person can only do so much. If you're going to be successful at higher levels of responsibility, you must be willing to delegate effectively; that requires you to trust your teammates. I think a big reason why many leaders are unsuccessful in this effort is because they fail to delegate the authority that must accompany accountability. If you're going to delegate responsibility or accountability to someone, then you must trust them enough to delegate the authority to accomplish their task. Too many leaders are comfortable delegating accountability but withholding authority. To all the control freaks out there, your failure to genuinely trust others will limit your professional career; it's that simple.

So, if you want to build trust, you must start by trusting yourself and your abilities, and that can come only from preparation, hard work, and experience. Then, you have to actually care about others and put them before yourself. Finally, your behaviors and actions must be consistent with what you say. The bottom line is that individuals trust leaders when they believe that they can accomplish more from working with the leader than by themselves. When you really care about others, communicate with candor and consistency, and delegate both accountability and authority, you will be well on your way to building what I believe is the most important facet of organizational life: trust.

● ● ● ● ●

Attribute #6: Self-Acceptance

One does not complain about the water because it is wet, nor about the rocks because they are hard.
—Abraham Maslow

No amount of self-improvement can make up for a lack of self-acceptance.
—Robert Holden

Introduction

Accepting yourself, including your flaws, is perhaps the greatest gift you can give yourself and those you lead. This section discusses self-acceptance, why it's important for self-actualization, and the positive steps we can take to begin the self-acceptance process—warts and all. It's a state of being that serves both our physical and psychological health and leaves behind the wholly unproductive activity of self-denial, projection, and constantly comparing ourselves to others.

SELF-ACCEPTANCE

Total acceptance of self in spite of weaknesses or deficiencies.

Why This Attribute Is Important for Self-Actualization and Leadership

According to Maslow, self-acceptance is foundational for living a healthy life and for reaching our highest potential. Without the ability to love and accept who you are, it is nearly impossible to truly love and accept others.

There are two levels of self-acceptance that support self-actualized individuals and help them reach their highest potential:

internal and external. On the internal side, self-actualized individuals identify with and accept their human nature in a stoic manner. They don't try to deny or justify their negative tendencies or traits, and yet they don't expend energy demanding that their nature be otherwise.

Maslow found that while self-actualized individuals accept the immutable, unchangeable aspects of themselves, they strive to improve, develop, and enhance those characteristics that are possible to change or improve.

I refer to the immutable aspects of ourselves as our *timeless traits*. These unchangeable aspects—our height, love of an activity or hobby, sense of duty, and the like—inform who we are. However, when we fall short in other aspects of our lives, aspects that could be changed, such as being jealous or jumping to conclusions, it is appropriate to feel regret and guilt. These are traits that can (and often should) be developed or changed. I call these *transient traits*.

For example, I have made peace with the fact that I am 5'8" and will never play in the NBA. There is nothing I can do about that. However, at times I can be reactive in certain situations (or with certain people), and that approach rarely leads to a productive outcome. Being reactive with others causes me to feel regret, and that inspires me to improve. Understanding and acting on the differences between timeless and transient traits is crucial for developing an objective and realistic appraisal of your developmental opportunities and can help determine what you need to accept or let go.

The other level of self-acceptance relates to our external world. Tara Brach (2003), author of *Radical Acceptance*, states that this kind of acceptance occurs at two levels: an honest acknowledgment of what you're feeling, and the courage to just *be* with that part of your life. She suggests recognizing those thoughts and emotions and then allowing them to exist without judgment. For example, you may be living with someone who constantly puts his or her needs before yours. When this happens, you may feel angry and resentful. Acknowledging and allowing these emotions to flow, without denying or repressing them, is key for living a full, healthy life.

Although accepting yourself at this level requires a focused effort and the realization that it is very much a *process* as opposed to a one-time *event*, it can be done! Below are some suggested strategies for letting go of guilt, shame, and regret, and for embracing total, radical self-acceptance:

» **Practice Relaxed Awareness:** Notice without judgment what you feel and think.
» **Grieve Losses:** There are people, dreams, and hopes that we've lost, and we should create the space to mourn their absence in our lives.
» **Stop Comparing Yourself to Others:** If you must compete, compete with yourself to be a better person, but stop comparing yourself to others.
» **Express Gratitude:** Journal every day, focusing on all the positive things in your life and the things you are thankful for. And watch Louie Schwartzberg's (2011) talk, "Nature. Beauty. Gratitude." at TEDxSF.
» **Serve Others:** When we are internally focused on ourselves and swimming in our own loss, regret, guilt, or shame, it's easy to get stuck. Reach out to others who are less fortunate and practice compassion and service.

At the end of the day, you must believe deep down that you deserve your own love and compassion. If you can't achieve self-acceptance for your own sake, then consider doing it for the other people in your life. What kind of love, support, and compassion will you be able to give them once you truly accept yourself?

• • • • •
ATTRIBUTE IN ACTION: CARL S. ARMATO

**Carl Armato is the president and chief
executive officer of Novant Health.**

For me, the process of self-acceptance has been just that, a process. I have come to realize that self-acceptance is not only the greatest gift I could give myself, but that it also allows me to live and to lead at a level that otherwise would not have been available to me.

Today, my interactions with others are grounded in a very high degree of self-acceptance, but that wasn't always the case. In fact, I grew up feeling self-conscious, as opposed to self-accepting. I had juvenile diabetes and knew early on that I was different. Back then, people with juvenile diabetes often didn't make it out of their 20s or 30s, and those that did make it often experienced amputation or blindness. In fact, I remember telling my new JV basketball coach about my condition, and I went from being the starting point guard to sitting on the bench because of his concern for my health. I soon found myself not only hiding this aspect of my health, but also feeling like something was wrong with me.

I am very thankful for my parents, who helped me feel more comfortable with my condition. My dad and I had numerous conversations where he encouraged me to be myself, to trust in my faith, and to focus on helping others with this condition. My dad passed while I was in my 30s, and during the grieving process, I completely internalized his advice and dramatically accepted myself. No longer feeling different, I realized that it allowed me to connect with others, both inside and outside of the healthcare industry, at a completely different and very authentic level. My mother has also influenced my perspective. She always told me to be the best me I could be and not worry about what others are doing. That advice still helps me today to focus on my organization, my family, and myself without the additional burden of comparison to others. That focus is a gift which helps me from getting distracted from what is truly important and impactful.

When leaders are self-accepting, they are able to interact with others with total transparency. I find that I am able to listen to and consider multiple perspectives. No one person can know all the answers, and that shouldn't be anyone's goal. My view is that leaders should focus on asking the right questions and having the humility and respect to listen to the responses. If I have an edge, I believe that it is my sense of self-acceptance, which allows me to ask questions, listen to different perspectives, and delegate authority to others to act on behalf of our organization and patients.

My dad started each day with the prayer "send me someone to help." Today, because of his influence on my life, my self-acceptance, and my faith, I truly feel grateful to be in position where I can do just that.

• • • • •

What's Next

This chapter introduced and explored the three emotional attributes of Actualized Leaders and provided practical insight from renowned leaders. Chapter 7 will examine the three remaining attributes that occur in the behavioral or "doing" domain: candor, flow, and solitude. Each of these characteristics will be defined and discussed, and then coupled with an interview from a respected leader to provide crucial insight into their importance in helping you become a better leader and achieving your highest potential.

Chapter 7
Behavior:
What Actualized Leaders Do

What's in This Chapter?

» Introduction
» Candor: Catherine Bessant
» Flow: Pamela Davies
» Solitude: Mike McGuire
» What's Next

Introduction

The final three attributes of Actualized Leaders are behavioral: what Actualized Leaders do. This section is critical because life comes down to what we do—not what we think, feel, say, or intend. Our actions speak volumes, and what we do or fail to do determines our path and our destiny.

Research into self-actualization and leadership identified three crucial characteristics of doing in which Actualized Leaders frequently engage: candor, flow, and solitude. As you will see in the following chapter, these three behaviors are tied to unique cognitive and emotional states and are easier to engage in when these states (be it cognitive, emotional, or both) are developed and enhanced. From a leadership perspective, individuals who speak with candor, find themselves in a state of flow (also called peak performance), and spend time in solitude are more effective, more intentional, and ultimately more satisfied. Each of these attributes is discussed in detail in the rest of this chapter, and the chapter includes insights and lessons learned from respected leaders in business and academia.

Attribute #7: Candor

A "no" uttered from deepest conviction is better and greater than a "yes" merely uttered to please, or worse, to avoid trouble.
—Mahatma Gandhi

A lack of candor is the biggest, dirtiest little secret in business.
—Jack Welch

Introduction

Candor, in the context of this book, reflects Gandhi's opening quote and not what is referred to in today's work environment as "front-stabbing" our colleagues (i.e., being blunt, rude, or outspoken). Rather, candor is a gift to others since such directness reflects sincerity and authenticity. Being deceptive, disingenuous, or sugar-coating the truth might help you avoid drama in the workplace by navigating around hurt feelings or conflict, but in the end, the practice is inefficient and time consuming and often delays inevitable changes or decisions. This section discusses why candor is important and what specific steps are needed to help you be more candid with others and reclaim your voice and authenticity.

CANDOR

The state or quality of being frank, open, and sincere in communication and expression.

Why This Attribute Is Important for
Self-Actualization and Leadership

Gandhi's opening quote emphasized that being honest and direct with others—displaying candor—is a way to honor our own beliefs and deepest convictions. Candor does not come from a place of bravado or being blunt—the intent is not to hurt or tear down. Rather, it is direct, honest, and authentic communication with another party intended to convey your true beliefs and feelings. Maslow said that practicing candor is so ingrained in self-actualizing individuals that they simply cannot operate in any other mode.

In his best-selling book *Winning,* former General Electric CEO Jack Welch devoted an entire chapter to candor. For Welch, a lack of candor is a sign that you are not being true to yourself, which just makes it harder to deal with reality. Bank of America Executive Cathy Bessant says that candor "honors your teammates" since it allows leaders "to cut to the chase." Jim Collins (2001) notes in his book *Good to Great* that facing "brutal facts" pays another substantial benefit to leaders: the right decisions become self-evident.

As I recounted in Chapter 1, it was my graduate school professor, the late Jerry B. Harvey, who changed the course of my life with his candor. He would not allow me to deflect responsibility about the failure of my marriage and challenged me to take responsibility. He told me at the time that his feedback was a gift I would one day appreciate. He was right, and his candid, sincere feedback transformed me.

Whether you're leading an organization or making decisions about a personal relationship, you owe it to yourself and anyone else involved to be candid. As you think about candor, here are some supportive points to keep in mind:

» Feedback is a gift.
» Don't assume the other person can't take it—is this something you have the right to assume?
» You are responsible for what you say and how you say it. You cannot be responsible for how others react to it.

» To truly self-actualize, you must act in alignment with your beliefs and values; when you are candid with someone, you take a big step toward achieving your highest potential (and may greatly help someone else on their own journey).

» Self-censoring is a retreat from fear and a step backwards. Life is too short; live it with courage.

Practicing candor is a choice that requires us to leave our comfort zones. However, the rewards outweigh the potential discomfort. For leaders, making this choice means positive movement on their journey to become a self-actualized leader; and for those they lead, the gift of candor has the potential to be life-changing.

• • • • •
ATTRIBUTE IN ACTION: CATHERINE P. BESSANT

Catherine P. Bessant is the chief operations and technology officer at Bank of America and is the lead director at Florida Blue, formally Blue Cross and Blue Shield of Florida.

Being candid with others is non-negotiable if you want to be an effective leader. I say that for several reasons, including a leader's responsibility to provide real-time, honest, and direct feedback to colleagues, peers, and direct reports. And yet it can be extremely difficult to practice at times. I think this is especially true in the southeastern United States where there is more of a culture of politeness that can—and does—interfere with our ability to speak directly to each other.

In the financial services industry today, more than ever before, being candid with others is a critical component to surviving in a hyper-competitive global market. I am responsible for leading the delivery of our end-to-end technology and operations across the entire enterprise, and there isn't the time or space for a lack of candor. It can be tempting to shy away from difficult conversations in the hopes that things will get better, but they rarely, if ever, improve. I have found that when we have the courage to be direct, open, and honest with others, we not only help our colleagues, but are happier with ourselves because we are living a more authentic life. My strong abiding belief is that we truly honor others in the highest form when we interact with them with candor and direct feedback. I believe there is a certain security in knowing where you stand with someone at all times and where they stand with you.

In order for candor to be the most effective, we must practice transparency every day, which requires vulnerability. If you truly engage someone with your deepest convictions and beliefs, you open yourself to vulnerability. When we practice vulnerability, we not only become more comfortable being candid with others, we are also better positioned to listen to and consider candid feedback from others. Candor not only makes our day-to-day interactions more efficient, it actually makes them more real. And when we establish and maintain this level of authenticity with others, we honor ourselves by living a more whole-hearted and productive life.

· · · · ·

Attribute #8: Flow

The best moments in life usually occur when a person's body or mind are stretched to their limits in a voluntary effort to accomplish something difficult and worthwhile.
—Mihaly Csikszentmihalyi

The basketball court for me, during a game, is the most peaceful place I can imagine.
—Michael Jordan

Introduction
One of the most significant dividends of self-actualization is the ability to become completely immersed in your work and enjoy peak

experiences, or flow. This section defines the concept of flow and gives some practical strategies to achieve it.

FLOW

An optimal state of consciousness where we perform at our highest level, often achieving more than we thought possible with seemingly less effort.

Why This Attribute Is Important for Self-Actualization and Leadership

The concept of super-focus and concentration was first studied in Western culture in the late nineteenth century by the famous psychologist and philosopher William James, who referred to this phenomenon as a "mystic experience" and attributed it to spiritual or divine intervention. He based the concept of mystical experience on what the Greeks and Romans referred to as "eudaimonia," meaning a happy and good life based on fulfilling one's highest potential. In her book *Big Magic*, Elizabeth Gilbert (famed author of *Eat Pray Love*) notes that both the Greeks and Romans believed the greatest human endeavors resulted from a divinely facilitated magical moment of inspiration. Maslow was uncomfortable attributing such experiences to a supernatural cause and chose to refer to instances of intense, ecstatic emotions and seemingly limitless horizons as "peak experiences."

Influenced by Maslow's work, contemporary researcher and psychologist Mihaly Csikszentmihalyi coined the term "flow" to describe a state of optimal or peak performance. It is the in-the-zone state we often associate with artists, performers, and athletes who become lost in their work or sport. No matter their origins, here are some elements common to these experiences of flow:

» Complete immersion in the task or activity.
» A sense of ecstasy that transcends our normal understanding of reality and performance.

» A total sense of serenity or peace.

» A sense of timelessness—losing track of time.

» A paradoxical feeling of being both more powerful yet more helpless.

Have you experienced flow in your life? Maybe you have found yourself in the zone while running, skiing, writing, or playing a musical instrument, or perhaps, while working?

Here's the tricky part—you can't find or create flow; it must find you. Still, there are some specific things you can do to increase the likelihood and frequency of experiencing flow. These techniques are covered in the next section.

How Flow Can Find You . . .

Peak experiences can make life worthwhile by their occasional occurrence. They give meaning to life itself.

—Abraham Maslow

Writing is the only thing that when I do it, I don't feel like I should be doing something else.

—Gloria Steinem

So now that you understand the concept of flow and Maslow's concept of peak experiences, let's explore strategies that will help you create the conditions to experience flow and rediscover your meaning and purpose in life.

To experience flow, you will need to take a few necessary steps. First, you should ditch your iPhone. Next, delete your Facebook account and get rid of your television. If you're lucky, flow might just find you and sweep you up in a thrilling moment of creativity and peak performance. But perhaps that's a risky and expensive route.

Here's a more responsible start. First, you really do need to disconnect in some significant way from those distractions so you can reconnect with your purpose and passion. After you've created the space for experiencing flow, you must engage in a task or activity that you care about and find intrinsically satisfying and rewarding. If you don't care about what you're doing, it won't care about you.

Once you've disconnected, created the space, and found something you enjoy doing, you must then stretch the challenge of the task to gently exceed your current skill level. In *The Rise of Superman* (2014), researcher Steven Kotler suggests that the gap between your current skill level and the challenge level should be approximately 4 percent. If the challenge is less than 4 percent, you are likely to become bored or apathetic. If the challenge is greater than 4 percent, then you may feel overwhelmed or anxious. Thus, the sweet spot for experiencing flow appears to be just out of current reach, but still attainable with a focused and dedicated effort.

There are certain arenas in our lives that heighten our focus and concentration. Some extreme athletes risk their lives to experience this sensation, but there are other ways we can replicate this acute sense of awareness. One is to take social or emotional risks. For example, you can choose to speak up when you disagree at meetings, or to let your guard down with a colleague or teammate. In the context of this book, an Achiever might choose to delegate an important task to someone else, or even ask for help; an Affirmer might choose to say "no" to a spouse or boss. Asserters might choose to trust coworkers or spouses. Getting outside of our comfort zones is exhilarating and also sets up the conditions for flow.

Add Complexity and Novelty

Another way to experience flow is to add complexity and novelty to your work environment. That may mean you take on another project, volunteer to take part in a cross-functional assignment, or mentor a junior colleague. There are also simple, almost mundane, ways available to add novelty to your job. For example, you might have lunch with a different group of people or change your commute to work. It does not have to be a major change: the point is to break habitual patterns and create a focused mindset for the day.

Another technique is engaging all your senses in the workplace. For example, the pleasant aromas emitted by a diffuser may help encourage flow when you're engaged in an important and challenging activity. Author and researcher Dr. Pierce Howard says he lights a candle in his office when he is engaged in writing to both stimulate his creativity and create a tranquil environment. Moreover, the scent of the candle serves as a do not disturb signal to his colleagues— which helps stave off distractions.

Here's a recap of specific steps you can take to increase the likelihood that flow will find you and provide meaning and purpose to your life:

» Disconnect from others and from social media.
» Choose a task, project, or activity that you truly care about.
» Gradually increase the complexity, or difficulty, to surpass your current skill level.
» Increase your sense of awareness and focus.
» Heighten your senses, including smell and hearing.

Individuals who are more self-actualized experience flow more often. In fact, Maslow stated that flow was so inspiring that it was payoff enough for becoming self-actualized. We all have access to flow, and it is my hope that the suggested strategies and steps outlined in this section will help you create the conditions for it to find you.

• • • • •
ATTRIBUTE IN ACTION: PAMELA S. DAVIES, PHD

Dr. Pamela Davies is president of Queens University of Charlotte and a director with Sonoco Products Co.

Getting into flow, or "the zone" as I call it, is too important to be left to chance. I believe that leaders perform best when they are in this optimal state, particularly when it relates to certain tasks.

We must take responsibility for making sure that we do our part in leading and living at this level as often as possible.

Personally, I operate in this flow state when there is a problem to be solved or an opportunity to be captured. I've noticed that there is an interesting paradox that must exist for me to truly feel like I'm in the zone. On the one hand, the problem or opportunity must be strategic and long-term, which often means that is it not a cut-and-dry issue. On the other hand, it must also be well-defined in order for me to perform at an optimal state. Flow guru Csikszentmihalyi references the apparent paradoxes associated with flow and the importance of managing these seemingly contradictory modalities for achieving this state. In my experience, this need for the problem or opportunity to be significant yet well-defined speaks to this paradox.

When I find myself in this optimal state, there are numerous factors that are consistently present. First, it nearly always involves collaborating with others. I have an extroverted personality and need to discuss, debate, and collaborate with my colleagues and team in order to become fully immersed in the process. Second, I often find that I lose track of time because I am fully engaged and never bored when I'm in the zone. Moreover, while I may on occasion feel overwhelmed by the magnitude of the issues at hand, I try to think beyond any obstacle to our work and focus on the possibilities. I am alert to even a hint of "barrier admiration" (becoming enamored or polarized with the challenges of a situation) on my team and am quick to address it. The same is true of sarcasm—there is no place for it on my team. To be in the zone, I must surround myself with big thinkers with creative ideas who are dissatisfied with the status quo and have a confident passion in our purpose. In the end, it is the exhilaration of victory that we seek.

Over the years, I have come to recognize how important the external environment is in helping to facilitate this optimal internal state. Our team is more effective if we can put ourselves in an offsite location, preferably in nature, with little or no distractions. I like for my work space to be clean, organized, and uncluttered, with plenty of natural light. Eating an ample supply of fruits, vegetables, and nuts helps to ensure that we are energized, focused, and ready to perform at our very best. I encourage the team to behave like athletes preparing for a big competition. Because, at the end of the day, that's just what being in the zone is for me.

● ● ● ● ●

Attribute #9: Solitude

I never found a companion that was so companionable as solitude.

—Henry David Thoreau

Whosoever is delighted in solitude is either a wild beast or a god.

—Aristotle

Introduction

Solitude is a crucial state for all leaders who want to renew, replenish, and perform at increasingly higher levels. Taking the necessary time to disconnect also allows the space for reflection, renewal, and planning. In Stephen Covey's words, it provides the necessary space to "sharpen the saw."

SOLITUDE

An intentional state of seclusion and disconnection from others that allows for reflection, planning, and renewal.

Why This Attribute Is Important for
Self-Actualization and Leadership

Maslow's research found that self-actualizing individuals transcend the normal need for affirmation, approval, and the company of others. In fact, he found that self-actualizers prefer solitude and privacy more than the average person. Of course, self-actualized individuals do develop deep personal relationships and friendships, but these connections tend to be with a smaller group of true friends as opposed to a wide net of social acquaintances.

Solitude is not loneliness. Rather, it's a tool that allows for connection with yourself and your sense of purpose. For Actualized Leaders, solitude is prized and allows for contemplation, reflection, and planning.

In Stephen Covey's book, *The 7 Habits of Highly Effective People*, the seventh habit is "sharpening the saw." Covey says that "time away" is critical for improving and sustaining high performance. He believes that our usual approach to personal effectiveness is to continue to "saw," or work furiously to try and complete a task. A more enlightened approach, one that is a habit of highly effective people, is to step back, pause, reflect, and "sharpen the saw" so that the project, goal, or objective is accomplished more efficiently and with greater ease.

Clearly, there are many benefits to spending time alone. We are more reflective and strategic and use the time to renew our energy, passion, and purpose. Tragically, most of us today have more excuses for avoiding solitude than in previous generations, due largely to the connected world we inhabit, which results in us missing our one opportunity to truly connect with our passion and purpose.

Carl Sandburg said that "one of the greatest necessities in America is to discover creative solitude." It is my hope that you will make spending time alone a part of your routine and in doing so discover the wonderful secret that solitude holds for all of us: when you embrace the down time of being alone, you will accomplish more with less effort and with greater passion.

• • • • •
ATTRIBUTE IN ACTION: J. MICHAEL MCGUIRE

Mike McGuire is the chief executive officer of Grant Thornton LLP.

Solitude is a critical part of my weekly routine and is foundational for long-term, sustained success. It is a must-have, not a nice-to-have, for me. Today, more than ever before, leaders are tempted with multiple distractions. Some are critical, while others are urgent but not important. If we lack the discipline and rigor to spend time in reflective solitude, it's easy to lose perspective on what's really important. When this dynamic occurs, our job begins to prioritize our lives instead of the other way around. In my experience, spending time alone not only helps me reconnect with my sense of purpose, it helps me retain control over my schedule.

Leaders must have uninterrupted time alone with no distractions in order to frame decisions, analyze problems, and reflect on opportunities in the appropriate strategic mindset to make the best long-term decisions. If leaders are constantly reactive, solving one problem after another, it's very easy to lose the strategic mindset necessary for asking why and instead focus only on [the] how or what.

At first it seems counterintuitive, but taking time away from your team and the job at hand will actually increase your effectiveness. Spending time in solitude is anything but downtime. More than just examining current or pressing issues, solitude also allows the time and space for reflection and planning. Every week I plan and schedule time to be alone and reflect. Saturday mornings are my time to focus my energy on not just solving problems in the present, but also looking ahead into the future for larger opportunities. A critical byproduct for me is that the more time I spend in solitude over the weekend, the more connected I am to my sense of purpose, and to my team, during the week.

• • • • •

What's Next

This chapter introduced and examined the final three attributes of Actualized Leaders related to behavior or doing: candor, flow, and solitude. Chapter 8 links these attributes together to present the 3 Sequences of Self-Actualization. When one cognitive, one emotional, and one behavioral attribute are all combined, the three unique sequences that result are crucial for sustainable effectiveness as a leader. The 3 Sequences of Self-Actualization are confidence, performance, and renewal. Each sequence is discussed in the following chapter along with corresponding illustrations that show why the sequence is important in achieving your highest potential.

Chapter 8
The 3 Sequences of Self-Actualization

What's in This Chapter?

» Introduction
» The Confidence Sequence
» The Performance Sequence
» The Renewal Sequence
» What's Next

Introduction

The last three chapters (5, 6, and 7) examined key details of the 9 Attributes of Actualized Leaders—objectivity, hyperfocus, optimal time orientation, courage, trust, self-acceptance, candor, flow, and solitude. Each of these attributes is associated with one of three domains: *Cognition*, how Actualized Leaders think; *Emotion*, how Actualized Leaders feel; or *Behavior*, what Actualized Leaders do.

While these attributes and domains are all collectively and separately strong indicators of successful leadership practice, optimal, sustained performance is possible only when they are combined into sequences. This chapter discusses the concept of sequences and, specifically, the 3 Sequences of Self-Actualization (see Figures 8.1, 8.2, and 8.3) that I believe leaders must master to perform at their highest level and, importantly, sustain that level of performance.

As you will discover in this chapter, each self-actualization sequence is built by combining aligned elements from the three previously discussed characteristic domains (Cognition, Emotion, and Behavior). These 3 Sequences of Self-Actualization are structured as follows:

» Confidence Sequence:
  › Objectivity—Cognition.
  › Courage—Emotion.
  › Candor—Behavior.
» Performance Sequence:
  › Hyperfocus—Cognition.
  › Trust—Emotion.
  › Flow—Behavior.
» Renewal Sequence:
  › Optimal Time Orientation—Cognition.
  › Self-Acceptance—Emotion.
  › Solitude—Behavior.

Please note that the 9 Attributes of Actualized Leaders are not only linked together to form the three sequences, one from each domain; these nine attributes are also linked to the 3 Sequences of Self-Actualization. The process of becoming a more Actualized Leader starts with confidence. Leaders must have a high degree of confidence (or self-efficacy) to take on the challenges they face and perform effectively in their jobs. It is crucial to note that Actualized Leaders often exude quiet confidence, marked with humility. Often, especially with Asserters, you encounter bravado and bluster. This behavior is often a way of compensating for low self-esteem and a lack of confidence. The kind of quiet confidence described here tracks with the kind of humble courage described in Chapter 6 by the Most Reverend Michael Curry.

Following confidence is the performance sequence, which is the result of quiet confidence built on objectivity, courage, and candor. The performance sequence is intended to describe optimal or peak performance, when someone is operating in the zone and performing at their very best. This sequence is built on developing hyperfocus for the task at hand, trusting yourself and others, and engaging in flow.

The final sequence is renewal, the sequence that ensures we create sustainable habits that allow time for rest, renewal, and reflection to avoid burnout. Personally, I most effectively engage in renewal when I have poured myself into a project and have experienced the performance sequence. For better or for worse, it is then that I often feel I deserve downtime and allow myself to truly rest without distractions or guilt.

Over the years, I have also come to appreciate that if I want to continue to do my best, to develop, and to improve, renewal most effectively facilitates that process. Taking a pause helps me center, refocus, and reengage with a renewed sense of confident expectation and inspiration. In that moment, I experience the 3 Sequences of Self-Actualization, then restart with confidence.

The Confidence Sequence

Confidence is quiet; insecurity is loud.

—Anonymous

Confidence is more than the fuel that drives productive behavior. It is the hopeful expectation of a positive outcome, whether that confidence is placed in one's own ability, or faith in another. Actualized Leaders are more fully integrated and balanced individuals and are more able to experience true confidence. I use the qualifier "true" to differentiate between both ends of the confidence spectrum, with arrogance, hubris, and false humility on one end and meekness on the other. Confident leaders possess a high degree of self-awareness that informs a realistic assessment of their strengths and weaknesses, and their confidence allows them to trust the decisions and actions taken by their colleagues and teammates.

The Confidence Sequence includes the Cognitive element of being *objective*, the Emotional element of *courage*, and the Behavioral element of *candor* (see Figure 8.1).

This sequence starts with objectivity, the true foundation for self-actualization. Without being objective and having the unobstructed view of reality that objectivity provides, leaders cannot make decisions free of hope-based bias or the cloud of their own leadership shadow.

The second sequence element is the emotional attribute of courage. Courage, as we've discussed in this book, is the ability to manage our fears and commit to venturing outside our comfort zones. Nelson Mandela's famous quote about courage is worth repeating: "Courage is not the absence of fear, but the triumph over it." Courage is what allows leaders to objectively assess an environment or their own limitations or strengths and to have the emotional fortitude to take the necessary actions, even if making these decisions is painful or unpopular.

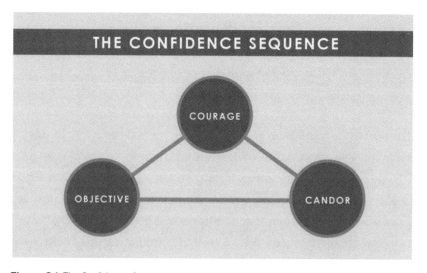

Figure 8.1. The Confidence Sequence

The third element in the Confidence Sequence is candor, defined as the state of being forthright and sincere in our communications with others. Rather than agenda-laden or hurtful bluntness, candor is about respecting the value of others without making assumptions about likely responses or reactions.

When these three attributes (objective, courage, and candor) are in place, you are more likely to experience true, grounded, and realistic confidence, which is the fuel necessary to propel you to your highest potential and purpose.

Developing Your Confidence

In a world brimming with arrogance on the one hand and insecurity on the other, confident leaders have a distinct advantage. So, what steps can leaders take to develop their confidence sequence? Here are some suggestions:

» Are you confronting the brutal facts of your current situation, or are you in a state of denial? Take the necessary steps to assess yourself and your situation with the clinical distance of objectivity, and make plans for improvement accordingly.

» Are you stuck in the easy and predictable rut of your comfort zone? If so, are you willing to get outside your comfort zone and act with courage to triumph over your fear?

» Are you frank and sincere with others, or do you avoid confrontation or sugarcoat the truth? Do you honor others with candor, or do you try to please them with watered-down versions of the truth? How do you think you (and everyone associated with your life) might benefit if you were always truthful, frank, and sincere?

If you felt confident you would not fail at something, what would you do? How would your life, and the lives of those you love, be different if you were confident enough to take that risk?

The Performance Sequence

The emotional reaction in the peak experience has a special flavor of wonder, of awe, of reverence, of humility and surrender.

—Abraham Maslow

The Performance Sequence is focused on the concept of flow. The term was coined by the University of Chicago psychologist Mihály Csikszentmihalyi to describe the state of being fully immersed in a feeling of energized focus and enjoyment in the process of the activity. Flow is characterized by complete absorption in the moment where one often loses track of time because of the profound sense of engagement in the activity.

In more popular vernacular it is often referred to as being "in the zone." To achieve flow, the task or activity must be challenging, but not so challenging (i.e., exceeds your skill set) that it creates anxiety. When you find this zone or "flow channel" between challenge and skill, you are more likely to experience flow or peak performance.

The performance sequence includes the Cognitive element of *hyperfocus*, the Emotional element of *trust*, and the Behavioral element of *flow* (see Figure 8.2).

Hyperfocus is the critical element of the performance sequence since it not only supports complete concentration on a current project or task (and avoidance of distractions such as social media) but also triggers the emotional (trust) and behavioral (flow) manifestations of peak performance.

Trust, the second attribute of the performance sequence, refers to the emotional state of having confidence in the character and performance of others. Trust allows us to delegate more effectively, and it is this additional time and space (or "runway" as I call it) that facilitates flow. Trust is also critical for managing and taking personal risks, an ability required for optimal performance.

The third attribute, flow, as noted above, is the state of being totally immersed in an activity. Flow allows us to perform at a high

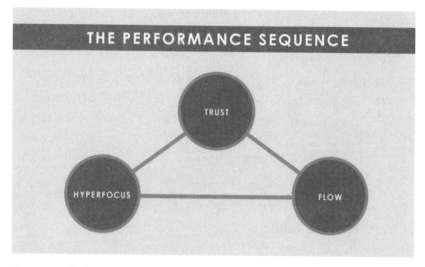

Figure 8.2. The Performance Sequence

level with seemingly little effort. We often think of Michael Jordan on the court as a quintessential example of this state. You can likely think of your favorite musician or favorite actor or actress who seemed to transcend the normal bounds of human behavior and leave you awestruck at an amazing performance. As a leader with these three attributes in place, you are more likely to experience a transcendent state of total immersion and satisfaction and (according to Maslow) attain a new, profound sense of meaning to life.

Developing Peak Performance

Clearly, putting in the time and energy toward self-actualization is worth it if the dividend is life-changing peak performance. Here are some specific steps you can take to develop your own Performance Sequence.

» Engage in hyperfocus to create the necessary space or runway to experience the transcendence of peak performance. You can begin the process by walking away from all social media, for example, and other nonproductive distractions like texting or *Keeping Up with the Kardashians.*

» Trust others and your own ability to swing for the fence and delegate projects and tasks to free up your space and time for your very best effort.

» Set up the conditions to allow flow to find its way into your life. When was the last time you felt totally immersed at work or home and completely lost track of time? How did you feel at the time?

The performance sequence requires discipline, risk, and vulnerability to live in what Theodore Roosevelt referred to as the "arena" of life. It is the realization, or actualization, of your highest potential and purpose. Although life is sometimes more difficult in the arena, the benefit is that life is more fun and exciting. Of course, engaging directly with life also means that you are risking failure, but daring greatly and failing is always better than never taking risks at all.

The Renewal Sequence

We must always change, renew, rejuvenate
ourselves; otherwise we harden.

—Goethe

The renewal sequence allows for reflection, reconnection, and recharging. From a human performance perspective, renewal represents a space or "sacred pause" from activity and engagement that allows us to face the day's challenges with vigor, creativity, and passion. Similar to a rainbow, it is the promise of something new and fresh just beyond the horizon.

The Renewal Sequence

The renewal sequence includes the Cognitive element of *optimal time orientation*, the Emotional element of *acceptance*, and the Behavioral element of *solitude* (see Figure 8.3).

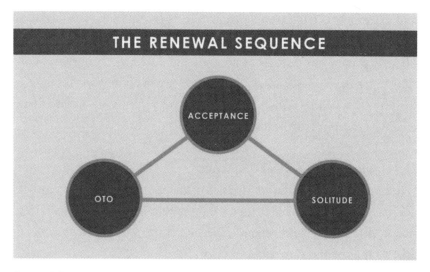

Figure 8.3. The Renewal Sequence

The renewal sequence starts with being mindful in the present moment, what I refer to as having optimal time orientation (OTO). This in-the-moment focus, without the burden of past regrets, current worries, or digital distractions (screens of all kinds), is required to fully experience OTO and the power of the renewal sequence to provide rest and regeneration.

The second attribute of the renewal sequence, the Emotional element of acceptance, refers to the "radical acceptance" (as characterized by author Tara Brach) of yourself. Accepting who you are, flaws and all, leads to true inner peace and tranquility. Carl Jung's pupil Isabel Briggs Myers (co-creator of the MBTI) stated that most well-adjusted people are those who are "glad to be what they are, or are psychologically patriotic." That's a very powerful notion; are you loyal to yourself and your true nature, or do you commit treason against yourself by disavowing your true nature and resisting self-acceptance?

Solitude, the final element of the Renewal Sequence, refers to intentionally seeking out time to be alone to facilitate reflection, relaxation, and planning. Although it may be commonly thought of as something to be avoided at all costs in our hyperconnected and extremely extroverted world, solitude is crucial for our ongoing growth and development. In her book *Introvert Power*, Dr. Laurie Helgoe points out that from an early age, we are encouraged constantly to develop social skills, but we are woefully inadequate at fostering "solitude skills" that protect personal boundaries, foster creativity, and nurture a life of the mind.

Developing the Renewal Sequence

Working harder and faster does not foster renewal. The creativity and passion that renewal brings are possible only if you are willing to pause, disconnect, and reflect. Here are some specific steps you can take to master the renewal sequence.

» Give yourself the gift of being in the moment by practicing OTO, and leave behind feeling guilty about yesterday or worrying about tomorrow.

» Are you a patriot to the cause of self-acceptance or a traitor? Do you honor your true nature as a patriot, or betray it like a traitor?

» Embrace solitude and take time to be alone, relax, imagine, and renew. Do you avoid opportunities to enter this quiet, still space? Do you use service to others to avoid this alone time?

In his classic book *The 7 Habits of Highly Effective People*, Stephen Covey used the metaphor of "sharpening the saw" to describe the renewal experience. The general notion is that by walking away from the treadmill of our hectic day-to-day activities to pause and reflect (i.e., "sharpen the saw") we will be more effective and, ultimately, more satisfied.

Developing the three attributes of the Renewal Sequence not only allows us to recharge and refresh ourselves, it also allows us to better connect (or reconnect) with our passion and purpose. When we pursue this goal with mindfulness we also open the door to personal transformation that helps us get beyond worries and regrets and connects us to a sense of purpose that is greater than ourselves.

To be effective, it is critical to understand the connection in the 3 Sequences of Self-Actualization. If you jump straight to the behavior—no matter whether you're trying to be candid, wishing to get into flow, or wanting to experience solitude—without the necessary cognitive and emotional elements in place, you won't be successful. You can be candid with someone, but if you are not thinking objectively or feeling courageous, you will likely overcompensate and come across as harsh or rude.

The same logic holds true for flow and solitude. Trying to experience any of these states without first developing the needed cognitive and emotional skills makes the actual behavioral manifestation and attainment difficult, if not impossible. Recommended resources for each of the nine attributes can be found in Appendix B. Enhancing and improving one or two attributes often has exponential impact. For example, focusing on being more objective doesn't just allow us to confront the brutal facts of a situation, it also creates the foundational state for courage and candor, and ultimately fuels the Confidence Sequence.

The full version of the ALP gives your scores on both the 9 Attributes of Actualized Leaders and the 3 Sequences of Self-Actualization. This tool will help you identify your greatest developmental need. If you score high in solitude, you are likely more introverted, and spending time alone to reflect comes naturally to you. You likely do not need to invest in developing this attribute.

However, if you score low in candor, your Affirmer style or more introverted personality may make being candid with others more difficult. This framework will not only allow you to calibrate your developmental endeavors, but also provides resources (see Appendix B) to help support your journey. My experience in working with leaders over the years is that if they enhance one attribute, the sequence will also improve, as does their effectiveness and personal sense of satisfaction. I would suggest you pick one attribute (or at the very most two) to commit to developing and improving. You may be pleasantly surprised at how much of a difference it can make, for you and your colleagues, at work and at home.

What's Next

Part Four of the book begins with the next chapter, Chapter 9. The final two chapters (9 and 10) are geared toward supporting your developmental journey as you transform yourself and your leadership style. The Transformational Change Cycle presented in Chapter 9 identifies the three key elements necessary for personal transformation: vulnerability, responsibility, and forgiveness. Allowing yourself to experience this cycle facilitates the entire developmental process and makes developing the attributes and managing your leadership shadow easier.

Part IV
The Transformational Journey

Chapter 9
Integrating Your Leadership Shadow and the Transformational Change Cycle

What's in This Chapter?

» Integrating Your Leadership Shadow
» Introducing the Transformational Change Cycle
» Vulnerability
» Personal Responsibility
» Forgiveness
» What's Next

To confront a person with his own shadow is to show him his own light.

—Carl Jung

Fear is temporary; regret is forever.

—Unknown

As discussed previously in this book, to reach their true leadership potential leaders must first be willing to confront and ultimately accept their leadership shadows. Although an Achiever's Fear of Failure Shadow, an Affirmer's Fear of Rejection Shadow, or an Asserter's Fear of Betrayal Shadow may bring up unproductive and ineffective traits in those leaders, don't think of these shadow manifestations as solely negative. After all, these potentially career limiting (or ending) shadow behaviors are also what psychologist Jung calls "learning gold" and as such have the ability to move us toward our ultimate potential. The key to mining this shadow gold and unlocking its power is to integrate it into our being. This process starts by understanding that the more self-actualized you are, the more often others will likely perceive you as a walking contradiction. And, as we learned in Chapter 2, that's a very good thing.

Integrating Your Leadership Shadow

Living an optimal life that achieves our highest potential requires confronting our darker side and making peace with the seemingly paradoxical aspects of our nature. We earlier examined the benefits of being a walking contradiction and how it is a wonderful compliment that highlights that you are, in fact, actualizing to your fullest potential by integrating your shadow. Engaging in these activities allows us to integrate our leadership shadow. When we integrate our shadow, we can begin to operate from a place of deep awareness and radical self-acceptance that will liberate us to work and relax without guilt.

We can be bold and reflective, candid and caring, outgoing and still. My professor and mentor Dr. Jerry Harvey, whom I considered to be highly self-actualized, once confided in me that he "poured his soul" into writing a chapter or article and that the experience so exhausted him he "couldn't even tie [his] shoe." He also told me that he was so nervous before a presentation that he felt physically sick, despite the fact that he was considered a dynamic and gifted public speaker ("story teller" as he liked to call it). Reflecting on these paradoxes in his own nature, he said, "When I made peace with myself and accepted my quirky nature, then I was finally free to enjoy life." What part of your nature do you need to make peace with? What will become possible for you, and those you lead, when you do?

Shadow work isn't easy and isn't always pleasant, but the more aware, open, and honest you are about your shadow, the more you will be able to integrate it into your entire being. And the more integrated you are, the more your shadow becomes a reservoir for creativity and passion. Remember, we've all spent our lives denying or ignoring these secret aspects of ourselves, so confronting them is painful. However, if you aren't willing to process and own unpleasant parts of yourself, then *they* will process and own *you*.

Maslow perhaps said it best: "You will either step forward into growth, or backwards into safety." Your ideal or actualized self is calling you to have the courage to step forward into the discomfort of growth, while your shadow is beckoning you to play it safe, stay distracted, and to stand still in your comfort zone. The choice is yours, and you really do have only two options: to step forward or take a step backward. Standing still is not an option.

When Jung was asked how to identify one's shadow, he remarked, "Yes, that is the question: how do you find the lion that has already swallowed you?" The shadow is elusive and by its very nature hard to pin down, especially when we deny it or project it onto others. As a familiar truism puts it: *we often fail to notice that which we refuse to observe.*

Four Ways to Meet Your Shadow

Our shadow likes us just where we are. The process of objectively meeting your shadow requires consistent, sustained effort and focus in addition to honesty and humility. This section will examine four ways to meet your shadow: writing, drawing, identifying patterns, and projection. And don't worry—you do not need to be a psychologist, author, or artist to effectively meet your shadow. All you need is focused effort, vulnerability, and a willingness to be honest with yourself. Having a sense of humor during this process doesn't hurt, either.

Before exploring techniques that reveal our shadows, bear in mind some common defensive mechanisms that work to keep us in what Jung referred to as the "fog of illusion." These mechanisms include total denial, total acceptance, or erratic oscillation between the two.

» **Denying your shadow** represents your shadow at its most effective. In today's StrengthsFinder culture, it is common to deny anything that doesn't fit your ideal self. This is a very common and tragic defensive mechanism.

» **Total acceptance of your shadow** lacks accuracy and objectivity just as denial does. Both total denial and total acceptance are extreme, inaccurate responses and equally unhelpful.

» **Wildly moving between denial and acceptance of your shadow** is unsustainable and difficult for those around you.

Writing and Drawing

Creative imagination, what Jung referred to as "active imagination," is an effective way to tap into our intuitive side, where profound awareness and insight await. Writing and drawing are two creative and insightful ways to help you identify your shadow. Tapping into this right-brained intuitive side allows us to access creativity and gain new insight. Invest in a journal or some art supplies. Imagine meeting your shadow, then record what you think would happen during the encounter. How would it make you feel? Let go of your inhibitions to draw or write this story, and see what happens.

Identifying Patterns

Shining a light on your shadow to identify patterns of negative or destructive behavior in your life can yield surprising results. For example, someone with a poor self-image or low self-esteem may look for faults in others to justify ending the relationship. Or you may notice that something that was once a positive trait—being thrifty with money for example—has morphed into something more extreme and negative. In this instance, you might have an unrealistic perspective on being frugal because of an underlying sense of scarcity or a negative experience from childhood that results in self-denial. Moderating this aspect of yourself would allow you to bring it back into balance and reestablish it as a positive, responsible asset.

Projection

Finally, pay attention to your extreme reactions. What do you tend to love or hate in others or dislike about the way society or institutions are ordered? Projection is the process of projecting onto others positive or negative traits that you deny or disown in yourself. In the Gospel of Matthew, Jesus taught about the ills of this dynamic and how it results in judging others:

> Why do you look at the speck in your brother's eye, but do not consider the wooden beam in your own eye? How can you say to your brother, "Let me remove the speck from your eye" while the wooden beam is in your own eye? You hypocrite! Remove the beam from your own eye first, and then you will see clearly to remove the speck from your brother's eye. (Matthew 7: 3–5)

Someone with a "wooden beam" in his own eye noticing and judging another with only a "speck" in his eye is the essence of projection. Pay attention to the faults you find in others as they are, very often, your own.

Steps to Integrate Your Shadow

In her book *How Did I Get Here?*, Barbara De Angelis expands on Jung's notion that our enemy is not our shadow. "Our real enemy is not the darkness within us," De Angelis points out, "but our rejection and denial of it. It is not by turning away from the Shadow side of our self that we find peace, but in turning toward it, knowing it, and embracing it as a long-lost part of our self." This section examines the steps required to more fully integrate our shadow into our whole self.

The word "integrate" comes from the Latin word *integratus*, which means "to make whole." The process of shadow integration means we learn how to own, and ultimately embrace, aspects of ourselves we consider negative (e.g., selfishness, laziness, lust). That's why it is important to understand the habitual things we do when we're on autopilot (in the fog of illusion) that feed our shadow.

Keeping secrets reinforces the psychological splintering or shattering (disintegration) of ourselves. When we keep secrets, we lie to others and ourselves, reinforcing the notion of "the other" that is often denied or repressed. This feeds our shadow and triggers a Dr. Jekyll and Mr. Hyde transformation. If we must always be right, thereby making others wrong, this behavior reinforces a notion of separateness which extends outward, thwarting or severing relationships with others.

By accepting our shadow traits, we are honest with ourselves and become better able to manage and integrate our shadow. When we have the courage to embrace this process of integration—and it is a process, not a one-time event—we begin to step into the light of our own authenticity. Ultimately, the work allows us not only to meet our shadow but also to access it for the gold that resides in the dark, including creativity, profound intuitive insight, and passion. When we meet and walk with our shadow, we can better manage the darker side of ourselves. As I often say, you can either meet and manage your shadow, or deny it and it will manage you. When we ignore our shadow we actually feed it and give it dominion over us.

Perhaps the wisdom from this well-known Cherokee Native American story says it best:

> One evening a Cherokee elder and his grandson were talking by the fire. The Cherokee elder told his grandson he needed to know that there is a battle raging inside of everyone.
>
> "My son," he said, "there is a battle between two wolves inside each of us. One wolf is dark and contains anger, envy, greed, guilt, pride, and jealousy. The other wolf is light and contains joy, peace, hope, love, humility, and kindness."
>
> The grandson thought for a moment and then asked, "Which wolf wins?"
>
> The Cherokee elder replied, "The one you feed."

Enhancing Self-Actualization—Integrating Your Shadow

Although no playbook exists to give you the steps to integrate your shadow and reclaim your potential, here are some helpful suggestions for your own self-actualization journey:

» Spend more time in nature.
» Belly laugh at least once every day.
» Express gratitude.
» Try something new that scares you.
» Practice mindful meditation.
» Say "no" when you don't want to do something.
» Say "I'm sorry" when you're wrong or have hurt another person.
» Admit your mistakes.
» When dining out, order what you really want and have dessert.
» Tell someone in your life that you love and appreciate them.

Meeting Your Leadership Shadow

If you are getting close to meeting your shadow and need support, here are some suggestions that will help you become a more Actualized Achiever, Actualized Affirmer, or Actualized Asserter:

Abundance: The Antidote for the Fear of Failure Leadership Shadow

> *Abundance is not something we acquire.*
> *It is something we tune into.*
> —Wayne Dyer

One of the single most important decisions you will ever make is this: *Do I live in a world of scarcity or in a world of abundance?* While many of us might explicitly affirm the latter, we often instinctively act as if the former is true. I most often see this dynamic play out with Achievers when the threat of losing or the thought of imperfection triggers their Fear of Failure Leadership Shadow. The purpose of this section is to explore the notion of abundance and how it can serve as a powerful antidote to the Fear of Failure Shadow and, in doing so, help Achievers become more actualized in their approach with others.

Scarcity vs. Abundance

In her best-selling book *Mindset,* Stanford professor Dr. Carol Dweck provides compelling research for the benefits of cultivating a sense of abundance, what she refers to as a "growth mindset." To illustrate this concept, she compares it to seeing the world through the lens of scarcity, or a "fixed mindset." When you see the world through a scarcity lens, you believe that your abilities and capacity for growth are set (or fixed) and that the world operates in a win/lose mode, which creates an urgent need to prove yourself over and over. In other words, the Fear of Failure

Leadership Shadow is activated and the dark side of Achievers—rigidity, narrow-mindedness, and pessimism—emerges, which almost guarantees they will experience what they are so desperately trying to avoid: failure.

By contrast, cultivating a sense of abundance with a "growth mindset" allows individuals to see the world in a win/win modality, where the success of others inspires, not depresses, you. Moreover, you begin to embrace challenges as pathways toward growth, to persist despite setbacks, and, most importantly for Achievers, to learn from and even celebrate your failures and imperfections.

Cultivating a Sense of Abundance
If you are an Achiever, you have many strengths in your favor: detail-orientation, organization, efficiency, and a strong drive for success and accomplishment. However, if you allow your Fear of Failure Leadership Shadow to manage you, you will likely never reach your highest potential, and even if you do, you won't be able to enjoy it. Here are some tips for cultivating abundance, the antidote for the Fear of Failure Leadership Shadow:

» **Confront your scarcity mindset**—As with so much in life and leadership, development starts with profound awareness. You must begin the process of cultivating a sense of abundance by acknowledging you have been living with a fixed mindset. Take note of the mindsets of those you surround yourself with as well; they can impact you more than you know.

» **Remind yourself that there is more than enough**—When you believe that there is enough to go around for everyone, you can feel yourself physically relax. Moreover, cultivating this perspective allows you to be inspired by the success and accomplishments of others, instead of taking it personally and allowing petty jealousy or depression to set in.

» **Embrace the world as win/win, not zero sum**—One of the greatest pieces of advice I received from my mentor

Dr. Dominic J. Monetta years ago was to remember that while some situations are zero sum (i.e., one party wins, the other party loses), I should never adopt that perspective into my overall worldview. The wisdom he imparted was simple but profound: know when to lean in and compete, and know when to step back and learn.

» **Offer words of appreciation and gratitude**—Telling people how much you admire and appreciate them and offering your own gratitude for what you have can be transformational. Over and over in my life I am reminded that when I put my ego aside and express both appreciation to others and sincere thankfulness for what I have without comparing myself to others, I feel centered and inspired.

» **Spend time in silent reflection**—In addition to allowing us the space to cultivate and express gratitude, time in reflection allows us to take stock of our blessings and to truly feel the abundance that exists in nature. In his book *Life, the Truth, and Being Free*, Steve Maraboli states that "those with a grateful mindset tend to see the message in the mess. And even though life may knock them down, the grateful find reasons to get up."

Perhaps the most important message in Dweck's book *Mindset* is that it is possible to cultivate a sense of abundance with intentional practice, including practicing the steps outlined above. Achievers have so much to celebrate; imagine the possibilities if you marry your natural strengths with an unwavering sense of abundance.

Actualized Achievers who have (mostly) conquered their Fear of Failure:

Redefine "perfection" as the effort not the outcome, self-disclose when appropriate, and stay out of the way of direct reports and peers.

Connection: The Antidote for the Fear of Rejection Leadership Shadow

> *We don't fear the unknown, we fear separation.*
> —Dr. Jerry B. Harvey

Affirmers are driven by establishing and maintaining warm, harmonious relationships. They are always there to listen to our problems, to empathize with our challenging situations (even if we created them), and to lend a helping hand. In many ways, Affirmers make work, and life, worth showing up for. However, when they sense conflict or a relationship break, their Fear of Rejection Leadership Shadow is activated and they become overly accommodating, indecisive, and conflict avoidant. Tragically, as Viktor Frankl points out in *Man's Search for Meaning*, that often leads to "paradoxical intent," which is experiencing the very thing we are trying to avoid. Said another way, Affirmers often meet their destiny—separation from others—on the very road (e.g., being overly accommodating, always saying "yes," etc.) they took to avoid it. The purpose of this section is to examine the notion of connection, especially connection to purpose, as a powerful antidote to the Fear of Rejection Leadership Shadow.

Connection: Internal vs. External

For Dr. Harvey, the fear of separation and rejection was very serious business because this fear represents primal, existential questions that we all face: Am I going to die alone? Who will take care of me if I get sick? What will my legacy be? From examining the dynamics of couples who aren't in love but decide to get married anyway, to examining work teams "getting on the road to Abilene," Harvey carefully explored how our fear of being separated or rejected by others leads to dysfunction, and often rejection, in our decision-making and behavior. By cultivating a sense of connection to our purpose, we can remedy this fear.

Too often we think of connection as having an external-only dynamic, such as our connection to family, friends, and community. In this instance, however, I am referring to an internal connection—a connection to purpose. Individuals who are willing to invest the time and energy into discovering their authentic purpose or noble goal become much less concerned about the approval of others. When you find and connect to your purpose in life, winning the approval of others becomes a secondary concern, if one at all.

The Role of Solitude in Connection

Ironically, spending time alone in quiet reflection and contemplation is the most effective way to discover your purpose. Affirmers often give all of their time and energy to others. And while that is an admirable quality, it is ultimately unsustainable. Too often, Affirmers sacrifice their true needs, wants, and values by trying to please others. Deciding to spend a weekend alone to take stock of or to reflect on your purpose cultivates a powerful sense of connection and confidence for achieving your highest potential.

Cultivating a Sense of Connection

If you are an Affirmer, you have many qualities to celebrate: loyalty, humility, empathy, and an intuitive sense that allows you to notice and appreciate the many nuances of human experience often missed by Achievers and Asserters. However, if you allow your Fear of Rejection Leadership Shadow to manage you, you will likely never reach your highest potential and purpose because you will have relegated that desire to someday in the future, after you've taken care of everyone else. Here are some tips for cultivating connection, the antidote for the Fear of Rejection Leadership Shadow:

» **Confront your shadow**—As with so much in life and leadership, development starts with the profound awareness that comes from confronting your shadow. Cultivating a deep and authentic sense of connection to your purpose must start with your willingness to acknowledge that your Fear of Rejection is preventing that from happening.

» **Examine your negative thoughts and fears**—Our thoughts are always with us. We often think through worst-case scenarios and catastrophize every possible outcome. Pay attention to your negative thoughts and the world they have created for you. Have the courage to test those thoughts and see whether they are actually realistic. Irrational thinking can only lead to irrational behavior.

» **Step into solitude**—One of the greatest challenges for Affirmers is to spend time alone. So much of this style is driven by a need for others and your connection to, and approval from, those in your life. In fact, oftentimes the thought of spending an evening or weekend alone seems selfish and can stir up feelings of guilt. Do not let that happen. Time in solitude is essential to renew, reflect, and most importantly, connect to purpose.

» **Practice saying no**—If you are going to achieve your highest potential, you need to create a to-don't list. We all have many demands on our time, and Affirmers often feel guilty when saying no. However, it's critical that we create space for us to follow our passion and purpose, and that means we will have to turn down many requests for our time and energy. Harvard Business Professor and strategy guru Michael Porter's insight on what makes companies great applies to individuals too: "the essence of strategy is choosing what not to do." The same goes for purpose.

» **Take action**—Affirmers need to make an intentional and focused effort to try new behaviors (e.g., saying no) in order to translate intellectual and emotional insights into a new way of being. Sometimes Affirmers suffer from analysis paralysis, meaning that we spend too much time in our own heads. Create the time and space to reflect, but make sure you are acting to actualize your potential and connect to your purpose.

It's often said that we come into this world alone, and we leave it alone. What would be possible if you reminded yourself that it's okay to live in it alone sometimes too because that's the only place where you can discover your potential and connect to your purpose?

Actualized Affirmers who have (mostly) conquered their Fear of Rejection:

> Start with a deep and abiding connection to their own values and purpose before connecting with others, are candid with others because giving feedback is a gift, and say no when necessary.

Assurance: The Antidote for the Fear of Betrayal Leadership Shadow

> *I can honestly say that nothing is as uncomfortable, danger-ous, and hurtful as believing that I'm standing on the out-side of my life looking in and wondering what it would be like if I had the courage to show up and let myself be seen.*
>
> —Dr. Brené Brown

Asserters are the rational, courageous, and decisive leaders who have a high need for power and like to be in control. According to the late Harvard psychologist David McClelland, they are the engineers who build our skyscrapers and the generals who fight and win our wars. At their best, they are charismatic and charming. Famous Asserters include Dr. Martin Luther King, Frank Sinatra, Jack Welch, Napoleon, and Serena Williams.

However, just like with achievement and affiliation, there is a dark side to power. Asserters have difficulty saying "I'm sorry" and asking for help. They are very uncomfortable letting their guard down and saying "I don't know," which often leads them to turn others away, although they actually crave connection. Their Fear of Betrayal Leadership Shadow leads them to be controlling and skeptical under stress and makes the very thought of being vulnerable painful, if not excruciating. In the spirit of full disclosure and transparency, I am an Asserter. I know this style and dynamic very well—the good and the bad.

Assurance is defined as a "confidence or certainty; vow, oath, pledge." This is where highlighting the Fear of Betrayal Leadership Shadow can be tricky. While Asserters appear to have supreme confidence, deep down they often lack the genuine, quiet conviction that comes from healthy self-esteem. As such, they often mask their fears and insecurity with supreme assertiveness, but underneath the bluster is insecurity and self-doubt.

Understanding the Origins of the Fear of Betrayal Leadership Shadow

Some Asserters often report feeling betrayed or out of control early in life. Other Asserters may have had a string of professional or personal (or both) wrongs or betrayals that cause them to be cautious and highly skeptical. The more betrayals we've experienced, the more we stay on high alert, which creates distance instead of connection. The bottom line is that the less predictable, loving, and stable our past relationships have been—including those with parents, teachers, friends, and lovers—the darker our Fear of Betrayal Shadow is likely to be.

Why Vulnerability Matters

Being vulnerable is critical because it allows us to connect with others in a genuine and authentic way. If we are unwilling to be vulnerable, we limit the quality of our relationships with others. Period.

It's difficult to explore vulnerability without considering courage. The word "courage" comes from the Latin word *cor*, which means "heart." Brené Brown describes it as "[telling] the story of who you are with your whole heart." Isn't that powerful? When was the last time you stepped into vulnerability to tell your story with your whole heart? What would become possible for you if you lived and led with this degree of courage and vulnerability?

Meeting and Managing Your Fear of Betrayal Shadow

» **Confront your fear of vulnerability**—This process starts with coming to grips with how uncomfortable it feels to let your guard down and be vulnerable. Take heart that you are not alone in this fear and that you have the power to step into vulnerability and survive.

» **Admit that it hurts to feel rejection, judgment, or indifference**—Acting like a negative response from another doesn't bother you is counterproductive. It's perfectly acceptable to own that feeling, but resist the temptation to build up walls to protect yourself. Sadly, we realize (often too late) that these barriers for protection have become the walls of our prison cell.

» **Forgive others, and yourself**—If you have a Fear of Betrayal Shadow, it is because you have been wronged. However, you must make peace with the past and forgive (not condone) others and yourself so you can move forward and step into your highest potential.

» **Remove people from your life who cannot be trusted**—You deserve better than putting up with others who betray your trust or act in bad faith. Clinging to these relationships will ultimately bring you down. Walk away.

» **Practice**—Getting comfortable with meeting your Fear of Betrayal Shadow is a process, and it takes practice. I can promise you that the more willing you are to experience vulnerability, the more comfortable you will become with it. This is not a one-and-done deal; take your time and give yourself permission to practice and to be less than perfect.

When we face our Fear of Betrayal Leadership Shadow and embrace the fact that we can experience vulnerability without the world falling apart, we regain the control we so desperately crave. By developing the emotional resilience to experience vulnerability, we no longer feel the need to run away from or shut down our emotions.

A quote from Brené Brown started this section, and I think it appropriate to close with another quote from her. She states that "when we shut ourselves off from vulnerability, we distance ourselves from the experiences that bring purpose and meaning to our lives." She reminds us that we cannot selectively "numb" the negative emotions—fear, anger, sadness, remorse—without numbing our entire being, including joy, love, happiness, and gratitude. Cultivating a sense of assurance allows us to have a confident expectation in the outcome of experiencing vulnerability. Whether the outcome is a positive, receptive response, or rejection, we can quietly and peacefully know that it is better to have been true to ourselves and lost than to have never been seen at all.

Actualized Asserters who have (mostly) conquered their Fear of Betrayal:

> Actively listen to others, readily say "I don't know" or "I'm sorry," express gratitude, and are willing to be vulnerable.

For many of us, in order to actualize our highest potential and connect to our unique purpose, we must experience a profound shift in the way we see ourselves, and our world. Anyone who has experienced true transformational change will tell you that the process can be an emotionally painful, and sometimes frightening, experience. After all, the journey requires us to challenge fundamental, often lifelong, assumptions and beliefs about who we are, what is important to us, and how others agree or disagree with this self-assessment. Make no mistake, this is not the kind of work to take on lightly since doing so requires both a willingness to leave your battered, defensive armor behind and a substantial amount of courage to put your security at risk and embrace vulnerability. Perhaps even more difficult, transformation requires that we have the grace to forgive ourselves and others.

So, what is the payoff for this effort? The first dividend of personal transformation is internal; you feel more settled and at peace with yourself and others. This self-acceptance then allows a more empathetic and understanding view of the world to take hold; you become less judgmental and critical of others. The external reward of this internal personal development is a better workplace and stronger personal relationships. I have never met anyone who has had a transformational experience and regretted it; they only regret not doing the work sooner. In order to become an Actualized Leader, you must be willing to meet your past so that you can let it go completely and step into your highest potential.

The Transformational Change Cycle

Change is usually a process, and not the sudden change in direction you might associate with a religious conversion or sudden decision to stop drinking or smoking (Devine and Sparks, 2014). The Transformational Change Cycle process presented in this book consists of three elements: vulnerability, responsibility, and forgiveness. A more detailed explanation of each element of the process follows.

Vulnerability

Vulnerability is defined as "being susceptible to being wounded or hurt." It's not surprising that we build defensive walls to protect us from the pain of reality. However, building a wall to shield us from shame or rejection also thwarts joy, happiness, and love (Brown, 2012). A wall also prevents us from experiencing the exhilaration of victory or the life-affirming feelings of true human connection. Brown uses the term "wholehearted" for those courageous enough to experience the uncertainty and ambiguity of vulnerability; these individuals earn the right to experience life as nature intended.

Vulnerability is the first element of the Transformational Change Cycle because dropping our protective facade opens us up to the feedback required to take the first meaningful steps toward personal growth. When we let go of who we think we should be, space is created to actualize into what we can be. Vulnerability is not a sign of weakness. It requires great courage to be open to feedback and to be comfortable with personal reflection—to reveal to the world who you truly are. C. S. Lewis beautifully summed up the concept of vulnerability and the price we pay if we choose to avoid it:

> To love at all is to be vulnerable. Love anything and your heart will be wrung and possibly broken. If you want to make sure of keeping it intact you must give it to no one, not even an animal. Wrap it carefully round with hobbies and little luxuries; avoid all entanglements. Lock it up safe in the casket or coffin of your selfishness. But in that casket, safe, dark, motionless, airless, it will change. It will not be broken; it will become unbreakable, impenetrable, irredeemable.

Life does not come with guarantees, so everything we do is a risk. Human connection risks rejection; authenticity comes with the risk of feeling shame; love risks a heartbreak. However, if you are courageous enough to be vulnerable, the reward is a full, well-lived, and adventurous life.

Personal Responsibility

Taking responsibility means being totally accountable for your response to every situation. While such an approach is empowering, it can also feel isolating and lonely. In *Escape from Freedom*, author Erich Fromm notes that for many of us it is easier to blame others than to take responsibility. In fact, Fromm concludes that given the choice between *freedom* (taking personal responsibility) or *dependency* (being a victim), most of us choose the latter. Such a choice is tragic since taking responsibility, as author Viktor Frankl points out, is our one guaranteed freedom—the ability to choose our attitude and responses to situations.

Personal responsibility serves as a bridge between vulnerability and forgiveness and facilitates ownership of the feedback we're given. Without this ownership and taking full responsibility for all our actions, self-awareness and personal growth ultimately cannot happen.

My long-time mentor and friend Dominic J. Monetta taught me two important and interrelated lessons in life. First, *you are totally responsible for yourself.* No excuses. Second, *you always have enough time for your number one priority.* Dom often says that our concept of time management is flawed. He asserts that we do not have a time management problem; we have a priority management problem. Here's a simple test: what do you find time for every day, no matter what? If it is updating your Facebook status, I'd suggest a serious review of your priorities.

Taking personal responsibility reaffirms our human nature to achieve and excel. When we try and fail, a powerful learning opportunity is available to us if we take responsibility and are willing to accept our share of accountability and blame that comes from owning our failures. Many famous and successful people—Michael Jordan, Oprah Winfrey, Thomas Edison, and Walt Disney—failed on many occasions. Each took personal responsibility and learned from the experience.

Personal responsibility is more than psychologically healthy; it also impacts us at a macro or societal level. In fact, taking responsibility is the price of admission for living in a free society. A recent Brookings Institution report (2015) stressed that if our country is to continue to grow and flourish, we must reinforce the notion of personal responsibility which has unfortunately, according to the report, eroded over the last few decades.

Taking personal responsibility is a compelling idea, but it's not easy to achieve. Like the other elements in the Transformational

Change Cycle, we put up roadblocks to our own success. We blame others and make excuses, even though we know that personal growth and success are just on the other side. Those who knock down these barriers get a variety of benefits including fewer negative emotions, the respect and trust of others, a sense of true freedom, and perhaps most importantly, a huge leap forward on the path to self-actualization. Here are some suggestions for reclaiming a sense of ownership for your life:

» Remember that you control your response to any situation—no one can make you feel anything.
» Accept yourself and your circumstances.
» Take responsibility for your mistakes without blaming anyone else.
» Care a little less about what others might think of you; their opinion of you is really none of your business.
» Forgive yourself and others, even if they haven't apologized.

Personal responsibility links vulnerability and forgiveness. It also means that sometimes you will have to shoulder both failure and blame. Another insightful truism that Dom taught me follows: *credit and blame smell the same.* If we are going to raise our hand to claim victory, we must also be willing to acknowledge and own our mistakes and failings. Remember, Babe Ruth was the Home Run King, but he also struck out more than anyone else. Brené Brown (2012a) reminds us that when we take personal responsibility for our own life, we get to write the ending. That alone should be all the incentive we need.

Forgiveness

The third element in the Transformational Change Cycle is forgiveness. Reinhold Niebuhr, author of the Serenity Prayer, states that forgiveness is the "final form of love." Forgiveness is most often thought of as something we ask others to grant us or others ask us to grant them. While these acts of forgiveness may be cathartic, a willingness to forgive ourselves is perhaps the most powerful act of forgiveness.

People of religious faith may pray for forgiveness, but no matter your personal or religious beliefs, forgiveness means that you must forgive the transgressions of others without condoning their actions. You must also be willing to offer forgiveness even if you do not get an apology in return. Choosing not to forgive someone is like drinking poison and expecting your transgressor to suffer. Forgiveness is a liberating gift you give yourself. Of all the definitions of forgiveness, I like Oprah Winfrey's the best: "Forgiveness is letting go of the idea that your past could have been any different." It's not personal, it just happened.

Finally, you have to forgive yourself. Making peace with your past means you believe you are better than your past. Understanding the different aspects and dynamic tension between yourself and your shadow will allow you to experience this kind of peace and live with greater intention and awareness, actualizing your highest self and realizing your fullest potential.

In her book *The How of Happiness*, Sonja Lyubomirsky refers to forgiveness as a "shift in thinking" that occurs when you let go of a desire for revenge, retribution, or harm to another party. In many cases, forgiveness will replace negative feelings with a sense of empathy, understanding, or goodwill toward the other party.

In addition to the psychological benefits of forgiveness, such as reduced depression and anger and increased optimism and empathy, clinically proven health benefits are also associated with forgiveness (Enright, 2001). These benefits include strengthened immune systems, lower blood pressure and heart rate, and improved quality of sleep. Perhaps French priest Henri Lacordaire expresses the psychological and physical benefits of forgiveness best: "Do you want to be happy for a moment? Seek revenge. Do you want to be happy forever? Grant forgiveness."

Closing the Transformational Change Cycle Loop

As a quick recap, here are the key points to keep in mind about the three steps in the Transformational Change Cycle.

Vulnerability

» Must be genuine and authentic.
» Remember, no guarantees exist. That's why this step requires courage.
» Becoming vulnerable and open to experiencing rejection, failure, and loss means we also open ourselves to joy, exhilaration, and authentic connection.
» Being vulnerable allows us to acknowledge and own our leadership shadow and opens us up to ongoing growth and development as leaders.

Personal Responsibility

» Own your current state.
» Taking responsibility allows us to reclaim our only guaranteed freedom as identified by Frankl—the ability to choose our attitude and response to any situation.
» Embracing this freedom allows us to stop blaming others and being a victim and to start investing our energy into positive change.
» Remember that vulnerability without responsibility leads to a victim mentality: a person who is open to being vulnerable ("wears their heart on their sleeve") but lacks resiliency.
» Likewise, responsibility without vulnerability creates a martyr mindset: someone shouldering more than their fair share of the blame without truly being open, empathetic, or connected.

Forgiveness

» Forgiveness allows you to let go of anger or resentment toward another person (or guilt toward yourself) and move forward with a renewed sense of purpose and clarity.

» Forgiveness does not condone the transgression against you; it simply allows you to move forward and to step into your highest potential.

» Forgiving yourself is making peace with yourself.

Change can be intimidating, but it is well worth the effort. Truly experiencing the Transformational Change Cycle requires courage, but take heart: the fear associated with vulnerability is temporary. The regret of not living a wholehearted life or actualizing your potential, however, is forever.

What's Next

This chapter provided a framework for experiencing transformational change and the necessary personal shift that is often required to accept and integrate your leadership shadow in order realize your highest potential. The last chapter, Chapter 10, will close with final thoughts beyond leadership. This review will examine the importance of gratitude, humility, and happiness, as well as finding passion and purpose in our lives. The book closes with a final challenge—the Obituary Exercise—to help you envision your highest potential and, in the words of Stephen Covey, "begin with the end in mind."

Chapter 10

Beyond Leadership: Humility, Happiness, Passion, and Purpose

What's in This Chapter?

» Humility and Cultivating Gratitude
» Happiness and Flourishing
» Rediscovering and Reclaiming Passion
» Living on Purpose
» A Final Challenge: The Obituary Exercise

For anyone willing to put in the work required to become an Actualized Leader, the benefits are easy to catalogue: more engagement from those you manage, greater job satisfaction, increased productivity for you and your team, and more enjoyment of your job. These are certainly important rewards, but the most significant benefit may be how your self-actualization journey enriches your life after you leave work at the end of the day.

After all, you were challenged during the self-actualization process to break down entrenched barriers that separated you from truly engaging with your colleagues. You learned to embrace vulnerability and trust others. You let go of worn-out excuses and took responsibility for your actions. And you discovered the life-affirming power of humility and letting go of petty jealousies and rivalries. Do you think there is any chance that these and other fundamental shifts in your familiar baseline personality or life-long behaviors will not follow you home?

This chapter points out a few of the more significant impacts your self-actualization journey is likely to have on your life, including perhaps the most significant of all, living your life to its full potential.

Humility

Humility is not thinking less of yourself. It's thinking of yourself less.
—C. S. Lewis

In his classic 2001 book *Good to Great*, Jim Collins showed that Level 5 leaders who practice humility and modesty are more effective than their charismatic, larger-than-life CEO counterparts. It's a finding that is easy to confirm by examining your own work experience. What characteristics do you most admire in a leader—whether it's a *Fortune* 500 company CEO, a community leader, or the head of neighborhood civic association? Your list of attributes may be short or long, but I'm willing to bet that one of the attributes you thought of was humility. Great leaders at any level are always the ones who are not threatened when they don't have all the answers and who continue to have a beginner's mind that welcomes a gap in knowledge as an opportunity for learning and growth.

So how do you continue your journey to become one of these admired, curious individuals? Here are some recommended practices that will help:

» **"Don't believe your own press release"**—I put these quotes around this first point because my mentors Dom Monetta and Peter Browning have both given me this advice. On the flip side, they have also cautioned me to "not believe your worst critic, either." Or as Peter likes to say, "You're never as good (or as bad) as your numbers." Celebrate your wins, but don't drink too deeply from the fountain of success. As John Dame and Jeffrey Gedmin point out in their *Harvard Business Review* article "Six Principles for Developing Humility as a Leader" (2013), a small sip can be energizing, but too large a gulp will impair your judgment.

» **Take an active interest in others**—Most people like to talk about themselves, so take the time to engage with those around you and discuss their thoughts, ideas, hopes, and dreams. Actively listen to what they say. People know when you are not listening, so put your own ego aside and really listen to others. As the adage points out, God gave us two ears and one mouth for a reason.

» **Stay hungry**—Success can either sharpen your desire for ongoing improvement or it can lull you into complacency. Don't forget that the world is full of other energetic, hungry, smart, ambitious people waiting for an opportunity to prove their mettle. Practicing humility will help ensure that you stay hungry, focused, and committed to improving your game.

» **Practice humility every day by saying (and meaning) "I don't know," "thank you," and "I'm sorry"**—You will be surprised by the results of this simple recommendation, both inside and outside the workplace. The practice will get you closer to your Actualized Leadership destination and ensure that you don't self-destruct with explosions (or implosions) of arrogance, pride, and vanity.

Gratitude

Gratitude is not only the greatest of virtues,
but the parent of all the others.

—Cicero

Gratitude, aside from being a characteristic that Maslow associated with self-actualizing individuals, is a practice that supports and maintains humility; it is also an excellent predictor of your happiness and life satisfaction. Years ago, I was a research assistant for a project that attempted to answer the question, *What factors predict happiness?*

The survey population, mainly a group of elderly people, was asked a series of questions based on common measures of happiness such as net worth, family relationships, and health. You can probably guess what the data showed after the results were analyzed. Only one factor in the study had a statistically significant correlation with happiness: gratitude.

That research project was twenty years ago, but many other researchers have come to the same conclusion—that a sense of thankfulness (gratitude) is the best predictor of happiness, satisfaction, and personal well-being. And here's an interesting point: gratitude precedes happiness. You might think that once you're happy, gratitude will follow. Not so. Happiness is not determined by how much money you have or if you feel well-fed and secure. Being grateful is what underlies happiness.

Here's an example from the happiness research noted above. One individual who took part in the study—a retired entrepreneur who was in great health—focused most of his energy on a 1970s business deal that had gone wrong and made him and his wife less wealthy than they could have been (they still were worth millions at the time). It did not matter that they were living comfortably with plenty of money in their retirement account. He hung on to the resentment and bitterness of that old outrage, and it continued to be detrimental to his personal happiness. Expressing gratitude is not only psychologically healthy, it will help ensure that you're happy—both now and throughout your life.

Happiness

Happiness is not a goal, it's a by-product.
—Eleanor Roosevelt

The word "happiness" comes from the Old Norse word *happ*, which means "good luck and fortune." Historically, happiness was defined as something that happens to you, but modern research has shown that about 50 percent of happiness is based on how you think, what you feel, and what you do.

In *The Owner's Manual for Happiness*, Dr. Pierce Howard revealed the results of his seminal research into happiness that connected individual personality to the ability to feel happiness. His findings suggest that individuals who tend to be more extroverted (e.g., outgoing, talkative, energized in a group or social setting) and less reactive (e.g., calm, serene, slow to anger) have a greater happiness "set point," meaning that all things equal, they are happier than the rest of us.

Sonja Lyubomirsky in her book *The How of Happiness* suggests that roughly one-half of our happiness is determined by genetics, or our personality "set point." The other half is determined by our thoughts and actions (40 percent) and by life circumstances—for example, wealth, possessions, family relationships (10 percent). Her major finding is that we tend to focus almost exclusively on the 10 percent when, in fact, we would be much happier if we put that time and energy into the other 40 percent—what we think about ourselves and others, how we feel, and the patterns of behavior and habits that dictate our lives.

David Richo in his book *The Five Things We Cannot Change* (2005) manages to put the entire topic of happiness into context with the "rules of life" that apply to all of us. These rules include the following: everything changes and ends, things do not always go according to plan, life is not always fair, pain is a part of life, and people are not loving and loyal all of the time. Richo says that to be truly happy, we must internalize these rules and view them as natural, not personal.

So, what can you do to be happy? Research has conclusively demonstrated that there are specific things we can do to be happier, such as expressing gratitude; nurturing social relationships; forgiving others; experiencing flow; engaging in religious, spiritual, or meditation practices; and partaking in regular physical activity. All these pathways will require work and perhaps some degree of self-control and delayed gratification. But for me, the price—whether it's eating less, exercising more, working diligently on expressing gratitude and thankfulness, or learning to apologize—is worth the reward of true happiness.

In *Man's Search for Meaning*, Viktor Frankl writes that too many of us ask the question: What do I want from life? Frankl suggests that the only way to find lasting happiness is to ask yourself: What does life require from me? What am I called to do?

What is life calling you to do? Are you heeding this call or ignoring it? Or will you snooze through another day that is calling?

Passion

Nothing great in the world has been accomplished without passion.
—Georg Wilhelm Friedrich Hegel

Most organizations spend a significant amount of time and money creating frame-worthy mission and vision statements, but I wonder how many organizations have considered creating a passion statement that conveys the emotional drivers for their business (i.e., *why* they do what they do).

Passion is defined and exhibited in many different ways: joy, excitement, anger, rage, lust. For example, a crime of passion is often characterized as a violent, tragic act brought on by jealousy, while a passionate love affair is used to describe an intense, exciting romantic relationship. In the context of this book, passion is the fire and energy that fuels our journey and defines our behavior on the way to self-actualization. Passion is why we get up early, why we work late, and why we persist in the face of disappointments and setbacks.

Passionate Leadership

Passionate leaders are driven by a nearly unlimited reservoir of energy that defines how they engage with their work. These leaders do what it takes to get the job done. Truly passionate leaders also inspire passion for their work in others. As seventeenth century theologian John Wesley said, "When you set yourself on fire, people love to come and see you burn." Passion also helps leaders weather challenging times and persevere even when the logical thing to do is to quit.

Passion and Success

In the book *If It Ain't Broke . . . Break It!*, authors Kriegel and Patler (1992) cite a study that examined the role of passion in success and happiness. The study selected 1,500 people who had just started their careers and then followed them over a twenty-year period. In the study, Group A consisted of 1,245 participants (83 percent) who chose careers with a high potential for financial rewards (the assumption was that even if the work did not engage them in a way that fueled passion, the participants would make up for the loss later in life, i.e., use their money to do exclusively what they wanted to do).

The other 255 participants (17 percent), Group B, chose careers more aligned with their true passion regardless of the potential financial rewards.

After tracking the two groups for twenty years, the researchers found that 101 of the original 1,500 participants had become millionaires. And here's the not-so-surprising part—nearly all of the millionaires (100) were from Group B, the group that chose to follow their passion, and only 1 participant from Group A, the group following the money, attained millionaire status.

What are you passionate about? Are you following your passion today? When you are at work do others come around to watch you burn, or do you huddle together around the warmth of the clock ticking toward 5:00 p.m.? As a very good book points out, "Where there is no vision, the people will perish" (Proverbs 29:18). When we live without passion we may not perish, but we certainly won't feel alive.

Purpose

So that's what destiny is: simply the fulfillment of the
potentialities of the energies in your own system.

—Joseph Campbell

To this day my stomach tightens when I hear someone ask "Did you do that on purpose?" Growing up the middle child with two brothers, we were often asked that question by our parents in the context of bad behavior, and my answer was usually yes. Yes, I meant to trip my brother; yes, I hid my younger brother's (Bert's) handheld football game because he wouldn't let me play; and yes, I was listening in on my older brother's (Wade's) phone conversation. Depending on the transgression, there was usually some negative reinforcement or punishment that followed this question. Hence even today at 50 years old, my stomach still tightens when I hear that question.

The underlying meaning of this question relates to our intention or objective: did we act on purpose? Sadly, many of us acted with greater intention when we were younger, even when our behavior involved sibling rivalry, than we do today when it involves our career choice, professional path, or life in general.

When I think about what it means to live from a high degree of self-actualization—being motivated to reach our highest potential and to perform at our optimal level—I think of qualities such as peak performance, objectivity, and even a little quirkiness. The other quality that comes to mind, perhaps the most important, is the notion of purpose. When we meet someone who has found their purpose we immediately recognize it. The person is passionate, optimistic, intentional, and intensely focused. Think about those qualities for a moment; they strike me as the ingredients for success in life and in business. And in turn, those qualities support optimal performance, which then actually reinforces our behavior in the pursuit and realization of our purpose. For me, purpose goes beyond mere intention and is closely aligned with its definition: the reason for which something exists.

Discovering Your Purpose

Joseph Campbell once said, "We must be willing to let go of the life we've planned to have the life that is waiting for us." That's a good first step: being willing to let go of what you think you should be, or what someone told you that you should be, so that you can become who you are intended to be.

Second, you must create the time and space to explore your gifts, talents, and passion. Sadly, many of us spend more time planning our summer vacations than our lives. Give yourself the runway to not only discover your purpose, but also to create enough momentum to take off.

Finally, you must be willing to embrace the fear that is standing between your current position and your potential. Deciding to live life with purpose will require changes, some small and some drastic. Making these changes will likely require you to get out of your comfort zone and to face your fears and insecurities. As transcendental poet Ralph Waldo Emerson framed it, "God will not have his work made manifest by cowards . . . always do what you are afraid to do. Do the thing you fear, and the death of fear is certain."

Are you living and leading on purpose, or is your purpose waiting to be discovered and actualized? What do you need to let go of for your purpose to find you? What fear must you be willing to face in order to pursue your destiny? Finally, what impact will you have had on the world when, at the very end, you can respond "Yes, I lived my life on purpose"?

A Final Challenge: The Obituary Exercise

Regrets, I've had a few, but then again, too few to mention.
—"My Way," Frank Sinatra

The Confessional Prayer in the Christian tradition urges followers to ask for forgiveness "for what we have done, and for what we have left undone." Whether you are religious or not, the admonition is a powerful notion—that we are responsible for both our sinful deeds, and for the righteous deeds we failed to do. If we expect to move beyond guilt and remorse and reach our highest potential, it's essential to examine how regret impacts our life.

Stephen Covey's classic *The 7 Habits of Highly Effective People* is again instructive for this discussion. His second habit, "Begin with the end in mind," examines the need for a long-term, win/win mindset. It's a game-changing approach to life because it forces us to look at the big picture and helps us avoid the many unintended consequences that occur when we choose to fight to the death to win today what really is an insignificant battle only to lose the war in the long-term.

Three Ways to Avoid Regret
Regrets are not typically born of risks we took that didn't play out as we intended. For example, owning up to our love for someone, only to have them reject it; or stepping up for a promotion and ultimately not getting it. No, what we usually regret is our absence of courage to take some action: not moving to another city when offered the chance or not professing our love for someone. Here are some ways to ensure this doesn't happen to you.

Lesson #1: Follow your bliss and do what makes you happy.
The most common regret is not pursuing your dreams and aspirations. So many of us take the easy, safe, or expected road instead of the path calling to us. We put our lives on hold to make enough money or to feel more secure, only to realize too late that 20 years or more have passed us by. The reality is, most folks look back and regret not daring to follow their dreams.

Lesson #2: Spend more time with those you love.
For a clear majority of humans, our family is what gives us true joy and happiness. So why is it that one of the top regrets people cite

at the end of their lives is spending too much time at work and too little time with their family? Yes, extra time at work may result in additional perks and more financial rewards for your family, but are these rewards worth being absent from both your children's and spouse's lives?

Lesson #3: Choose to be happy with a grateful heart
with whatever you have, wherever you are.
Finally, research demonstrates that many of us will look back and wish we would have let ourselves be happier. For me personally, this really hits home. I would say that I am reasonably happy but always looking for the next challenge or opportunity. I believe that growth and development are important, but when they come at the cost of always feeling unsettled and thinking "what's next?," I'm reminded that the question I should be asking myself is "what's the point?" Happiness really is a choice, and many of us are trapped in the notion that more stuff will provide it. It doesn't.

The Obituary Exercise

A powerful self-actualizing exercise is to write your obituary. Known as "The Obituary Exercise," this activity really brings home Covey's point about beginning with the end, the ultimate end, in mind. I have facilitated this exercise many times, and very few people want accomplishments or success alone to define them. Most of us want to be remembered as loving partners and parents, loyal friends, and responsible citizens. Unfortunately, most of our lives don't consistently reflect these values since we are all guilty of putting an inordinate amount of our time and energy into accomplishments and success, often at the expense of our families and communities.

Realistically, no one is perfect, and therefore we are all likely to have some regrets in our lives. But I believe if we live with "the end in mind," we would be more likely to follow our dreams, work less, love more, and allow in our lives only others who lift us up and make us happy. The good news in the Actualized Performance Cycle is that personal transformation can occur when you make a commitment to lead, and live, in a different way. No matter your past behaviors, there is time to change and claim your future.

If you wrote your obituary today, what would it say? What have you left undone? Are your regrets too few to mention or too numerous to count and too painful to acknowledge?

Final Thoughts

It is my sincere hope that this process, both reading the book and applying your personal ALP results, has been insightful for you. The process of meeting our darker side, our leadership shadow, can sometimes be upsetting. As stated earlier, true self-awareness does not comfort—it disturbs. However, it is within this disturbance that we are afforded an opportunity for growth and development. And it is in this process of growing that we can make peace with our past and position ourselves to step into our future, and our highest potential. There are many competing models for understanding the process of leadership and for optimizing your approach. Many approaches focus on specific tactics to use, or avoid, in order to more effectively influence others and deliver results. The Actualized Performance Cycle is focused on improving results and team member engagement, but the approach is very personal. The essential idea put forth in the book follows: The more self-actualized you are, the less you (and your coworkers) will experience your leadership shadow. Likewise, the less self-actualized you are, the more you (and your coworkers) will experience your leadership shadow, which increases the probability that you will experience the tragic irony of the human condition: paradoxical intent. I hope that you will take the time to give your leadership shadow the attention it deserves, so that you manage it more effectively and actualize your highest potential.

Appendix A
The ALP Styles at a Glance

LEADER STYLE	ACHIEVER	AFFIRMER	ASSERTER
MOTIVATION	Achievement	Affiliation	Power
DESCRIPTION	Organized Focused Disciplined Detail-Oriented	Friendly Warm Empathetic Loyal	Candid Decisive Rational Strategic
LEADERSHIP SHADOW	Fear of Failure	Fear of Rejection	Fear of Betrayal
SHADOW TENDENCIES	Narrow-minded Rigid Cautious "Micromanager"	Anxious Conflict-avoidant Naïve Accommodating	Controlling Arrogant Blunt Condescending
IMPACT ON OTHERS	"Detached" Group Culture	"Dramatic" Group Culture	"Dependent" Group Culture

Appendix B

Developmental Resources

Attribute	Book	Article	Program/Video
Objective Degree to which your judgment is based on facts and not influenced by personal feelings or preferences.	Confronting Reality: Doing What Matters to Get Things Right *by: Larry Bossidy & Ram Charan*	Level 5 Leadership	How to Face Reality
Hyperfocus Degree to which you consistently engage in an intense form of mental concentration.	Hyperfocus: The New Science of Attention, Productivity, and Creativity *by: Chris Bailey*	The Focused Leader	The Focus and Attention Program
Optimal Time Orientation (OTO) Degree to which you have a balanced sense of time and live primarily in the present.	Mindfulness: A practical guide to finding peace in a frantic world *by: Danny Penman and J. Mark G. Williams*	Practicing Mindfulness Throughout Your Work Day	All It Takes Is 10 Minutes of Mindfulness
Courage Degree to which you are willing to do something that frightens you in order to act in accordance with your beliefs.	Daring Greatly: How the Courage to Be Vulnerable Transforms the Way We Live, Love, Parent, and Lead *by: Brené Brown*	Have the Courage To Be Direct	The Gift and Power of Emotional Courage
Trust Degree to which you trust others, yourself, and maintain a confident expectation in a productive and positive outcome.	Trust and Betrayal in the Workplace *by: Dennis & Michelle Reina*	Want Your Employees to Trust You? Show You Trust Them	The Anatomy of Trust: Brené Brown
Acceptance Degree to which you totally and completely accept yourself—flaws, limitations, the aging process and all.	Radical Acceptance *by: Tara Brach*	To Recover from Failure, Try Some Self-Compassion	Unconditional Self-Acceptance
Candor Degree to which you are open, honest, frank, and sincere in your communications with others.	Radical Candor *by: Kim Scott*	A Culture of Candor	Radical Candor
Flow Degree to which you consistently engage in peak performance "in the zone," where you are fully engaged.	Flow: The Psychology of Optimal Experience *by: Mihaly Csikszentmihalyi*	Create A Work Environment That Fosters Flow	The Secret to Flow: Mihaly Csikszentmihalyi
Solitude Degree to which you are comfortable being alone to proactively plan, reflect, and renew.	Lead Yourself First: Inspiring Leadership Through Solitude *by: Raymond M. Kethledge*	The Surprising Benefits of Solitude	The Art of Alone: Intentional Solitude

Appendix C
Technical Statement: Reliability and Validity for the ALP

The purpose of Appendix C is to demonstrate the validity and reliability of the Actualized Leader Profile (ALP) survey, both the Long Form and the Short Form versions.[1] The ALP is a 57-item self-report assessment that measures an individual's dominant motive need, corresponding leadership style, and leadership "shadow." The statistical analyses support a four-factor model of human motivation and leader behavior. The four-factor model in the PCFA analysis includes Achievement, Affiliation, Power, and Self-Actualization.

The ALP is based primarily on the seminal works in human motivation of David McClelland (1987) and Abraham Maslow (1954). McClelland's research into human motivation focused on the internal motive needs or "drivers" that direct and sustain human behavior: Achievement, Affiliation, and Power. In addition to McClelland's research, the ALP framework includes Abraham Maslow's concept of "self-actualization" as the fourth motive need and a modifier of the first three motive needs. In this current research effort, "self-actualization" was determined to be a fourth, unique motive need along with the three identified by McClelland, but the ALP conceptualizes this scale as a modifier of the first three needs (measuring intensity of the other needs, and thus the participant's level of reactivity).

Validity for the ALP was established using a Principal Components Factor Analysis (PCFA) to ascertain both the number

---

1 The ALP short-form (Free ALP), included in this book, is a subset of the larger ALP long-form assessment. The word-pair section of this technical report provides the statistical information and reliability for these items.

of factors (four) and the factor loadings for each survey item on the four scales. A four-factor model with eigenvalues greater than 1.0 was generated, and survey items were reduced from 40 to 20 based on the factor loading scores. Eigenvalues ranged from 14.13 to 1.91, and accounted for 44% of the observed variance. The reliability for the ALP was estimated by assessing the internal consistency of the survey items for each of the four scales (i.e., Achievement, Affiliation, Power, and Self-Actualization) by calculating Cronbach's alpha for each scale item. The standardized item Cronbach's alpha for the four scales ranged from .781 to .857. The research effort is summarized, and conclusions are drawn with specific implications for leadership development.

INTRODUCTION

The Actualized Leader Profile (ALP) is a 57-item self-report leadership assessment that measures leader style based on the intensity of the participant's dominant motive need. The ALP is based primarily on seminal works in human motivation (Maslow, 1954; McClelland, 1987). The theoretical framework for the ALP has been enhanced with the work of Viktor Frankl and Carl Jung.

McClelland's research into human motivation focused on the internal motive needs or "drivers" that direct and sustain human behavior. He identified three motive needs that propel individual behavior: Achievement, Affiliation, and Power. Although every individual is a unique combination of all three, usually one motive need is dominant, particularly under stress (McClelland, 1987). In addition to McClelland's research, the ALP framework includes Abraham Maslow's concept of "self-actualization" as the fourth need, and a modifier of the first three motive needs. Maslow loosely defined "self-actualization" in his famous hierarchy of needs as the highest need that can emerge to drive human behavior, and this need represents our drive to reach our highest potential and ultimate purpose (Maslow, 1954). In this current research effort, "self-actualization" was determined to be a fourth, unique motive need along with the three motive needs identified by McClelland, but the ALP uses it as a modifier as opposed to a fourth style, meaning that it measures the intensity of the other needs, and the participant's level of reactivity. This conceptual approach and the resulting scoring model in the ALP help the assessment to determine both the intensity of this need in driving behavior for the participant, and to predict how reactive the individual is likely to be under stress both in terms of intensity of behavior (i.e., Light, Medium, or Dark) and in frequency of their Leadership Shadow activation (i.e., Less Often, Moderately, or More Often). Table C.1 provides an overview of the three motive needs and their relationship to leader behaviors.

The higher a participant's score in self-actualization, the more resilient and less reactive he or she is likely to be under stress. Conceptualizing self-actualization as a modifier, as opposed to a fourth style, is supported in the literature (Spreier, Fontaine, & Malloy, 2006) that discussed the differences between McClelland's concept of "personal power" and a more self-actualized, others-based approach to power, "social power." Therefore, the explicit goal of the ALP is for each participant to focus his or her developmental efforts on becoming more self-actualized in his or her style, Achievement, Affiliation, or Power.

The impulsive, reactive side of leader behavior is referred to as the "Leadership Shadow," and this concept is based on the seminal work of Carl Jung (1969), who in the mid-1920s first coined the term "shadow" to refer to the darker, instinctual side of individual personality that is often activated under stress. According to Jung,

Table C.1. Motive Needs and Their Relationship to Leader Behaviors

Motive Need	Leadership Style	Leadership Shadow
Achievement	Achiever	Fear of Failure
Affiliation	Affirmer	Fear of Rejection
Power	Asserter	Fear of Betrayal

the Shadow exists at multiple levels: personal and collective. The ALP focuses on the personal level, and refines it even further as the extreme or "darker" side of the first three motive needs. This delineation is crucial because a unique, reactive, or "shadow" side is associated with each motive need. Under stress, when an individual is lower in self-actualization, he or she is more likely to engage in negative, "shadow" behaviors.

The 57-item self-report ALP assessment scale is divided into three sections. Section one contains 20 survey items, five (5) items for each of the four (4) scales (i.e., Achievement, Affiliation, Power, and Self-Actualization). The results of the factor loading analyses using PCFA for item retention are discussed. Section two consists of 10 word-pair choices where the participant is asked to choose one word from each pair that is most descriptive of their style at work. Finally, three (3) survey items for each of the nine (9) attributes scales (n=27) were developed and will be assessed for validity in the subsequent statistical analysis of the ALP when a sufficient data set is developed. The results of the assessment's evaluation, and the implications for leadership development, are discussed.

THEORETICAL FRAMEWORK

The ALP is based on an effort to synthesize and integrate various and competing models of human behavior as they relate to leadership and leader behavior, and these theories and models will be presented in this section. The psychologists, researchers, and human development philosophers providing the foundation for the ALP are Viktor Frankl, David McClelland, Carl Jung, and Abraham Maslow. The ALP framework represents an attempt to distill, synthesize, and integrate these various and, at times, competing models and theories into one integrated framework. Although an obvious cornerstone for this model is the seminal work of Abraham Maslow who coined the term "self-actualization" as it relates to human potential and peak performance, the framework actually starts with the work of Viktor Frankl. Frankl is the author of *Man's Search for Meaning* and has influenced an untold number of researchers, psychologists, and philosophers. His philosophical foundation provides the basis for the ALP and the *Actualized Performance Cycle* presented at the paper's conclusion.

Viktor Frankl: Personal Freedom and Paradoxical Intent

In his best-selling book *Man's Search for Meaning*, Austrian psychoanalyst Viktor Frankl (1946) discussed the horrors of his experience as a prisoner in concentration camps during World War II. It was in these hellish conditions that he came to realize that everything can be taken from us but one thing: *our freedom to choose our response to any situation*. This insight provides the first pillar and a basic assumption of our model: You are free to choose your response and your attitude to anyone and any situation.

But, can we avoid some suffering, or are we destined to lead in ways that damage ourselves and others? Perhaps Frankl's most powerful contribution is his concept of "paradoxical intent," which is as follows: *the more we fear something, the more likely we are to experience it.*

Let that insight sink in for just a moment. That observation reminds us of some of the tragic ironies of the human condition. The more we fear being alone, or being rejected, or failing in an endeavor, the more likely we will experience what we so fear. In his classic *The Abilene Paradox*, the late Jerry B. Harvey (1974) refers to this concept as a "Paradox within a Paradox." Both Frankl and Harvey warn us that the sad, tragic irony of the human condition is that the more we fear something, the more likely we are to think (obsess), feel (fear) and do (counterproductive behaviors) things that almost guarantee we will experience that which we so fear. From a leadership perspective, consider a high *Achiever* who is low in Self-Actualization. At his or her best, the Achiever is well-organized, detail-oriented, and efficient. However, under stress, for example due to a lack of clear direction or increased ambiguity, he or she will begin to engage in "shadow" Achiever behaviors, such as becoming rigid, narrow-minded, and the classic "micromanager." Over time, this cycle will limit the individual's upward mobility in a managerial role, fulfilling paradoxical intent.

Viktor Frankl's insight establishes the foundation for the ALP and the *Actualized Performance Cycle*. First, you always have the freedom to choose your response to a situation or person. Second, the more you fear something, the more likely you are to experience it. While these assertions may seem at first glance to be self-evident or even depressing, they are actually liberating when considered in the context of Maslow's concept of "self-actualization," which we will review shortly. Before doing so, let's turn our attention to human motivation and the motive needs or "drivers" that propel our behavior. In this endeavor, we will review the seminal work of David McClelland.

David McClelland: Human Motivation and the Three Motive Needs

Many behavioral science theories attempting to explain human motivation—what drives us to do what we do—have been proposed over the last 100 years. Some researchers have focused on the internal needs of individuals that drive our behavior, while other researchers have examined the context and process by which we exert effort, and the expectations we have on successfully being rewarded. Although the works of Maslow (1954) and Herzberg, Mausner, and Snyderman (1959) remain extremely popular, perhaps no other researcher has been more influential than David McClelland and his three-need or "Acquired Need" theory of human motivation.

The word motivation comes from the Latin word *movere* which means "to move" or "to stir." A need may be best thought of as an "internal state that makes a certain outcome appear attractive" (Robbins & Coulter, 2011). So, when we think of motive needs, also referred to as "drivers," we are simply examining the internal states that drive or stir our behavior in an attempt to satisfy this need (e.g., our desire for safety, the need for relationships and connection to others, our desire for control, etc.). There are a number of very influential theorists through the years who have informed our thinking in this area, including Yale psychologist Clayton Alderfer's ERG Theory (1972), and Frederick Herzberg's "Two-factor theory" (1959). It could be argued that no one has been more influential in describing what motivates or drives us to do the things that we do than the late Harvard psychologist David McClelland. McClelland (1987) identified three motive needs or drivers that propel our behavior: *Achievement, Affiliation,* and *Power.*

Achievers, those with a high need for achievement, are driven for success, improvement, and accomplishment. They are primarily concerned with expertise and competence, and are detail-oriented, focused, and very well-organized. These individuals are efficient, rules- and process-oriented, and prefer consistency and predictability. Under stress, however, their Leadership Shadow is triggered and *Achievers* become narrow-minded and rigid, transforming into the classic "micromanager" which has been discussed briefly and will be examined in greater detail during the review of Carl Jung.

Affirmers, those with a high need for affiliation, are warm and friendly, and are more focused on interpersonal relationships and harmony than results and outcomes. They are primarily concerned with their connection to, and acceptance from, others. These individuals are loyal, trusting, and empathetic. Under stress, when their Leadership Shadow is triggered, these individuals become overly accommodating, avoiding confrontation and allowing others to take advantage of them.

Asserters, those with a high need for power, are candid, decisive, and courageous risk-takers. They are often viewed as "natural" leaders who challenge the status quo and drive results. *Asserters* are primarily concerned with control and can be skeptical and slow to trust others. Under stress, when their Leadership Shadow is triggered, they become controlling, autocratic, and condescending, often manipulating or intimidating others to get their way.

The PCFA demonstrated a four-factor model, with Self-Actualization being the fourth need with an eigenvalue greater than 1.00. A review of Abraham Maslow's work and theory of Self-Actualization and "Hierarchy of Needs" will be discussed as a modifier of the first three needs. Before reviewing Maslow's work, let's examine Jung's influential work in the human psyche, and the implications for understanding leader behaviors under stress.

Carl Jung: Leadership Shadows

Perhaps no one in the last 100 years has been more influential to Western culture than Carl Jung. From his theories of personality type ("introversion" and "extroversion") that led to the MBTI, to his concepts of the "collective unconscious," "archetypes," and "synchronicity," one could make a compelling argument that Jung's influence over the last 100 years is without a contemporary equal. An untold number of therapists and researchers have built their entire practices, and careers, on his concepts and frameworks. And it is Jung's concept of the "shadow" that is critical for understanding how normally positive traits (e.g., organized and efficient) can become negative (e.g., rigid and inflexible) under stress.

The "shadow" is Jung's concept of the dark, unconscious aspect that resides within each of us. Jung believed that in addition to an individual's shadow, there is also a collective unconscious that is essentially the repository or unconscious DNA of human history, varying by culture. Although he was convinced that the collective shadow had an enormous impact on human behavior in the present, our focus will be to further refine his notion of the "personal shadow" by looking specifically at leader behaviors under stress, and how normally positive characteristics and traits can and do become dysfunctional or outright destructive.

The Shadow has been defined as the dark, rejected, instinctual side of ourselves that we deny or repress. Impulses such as rage, lust, greed, and jealousy reside in the Shadow, but so too do creativity, passion, and profound insight. The more aware, open, and honest you are about your Shadow, the more integrated it becomes into your entire being. And the more integrated you are, the more your Shadow becomes a reservoir for creativity and passion.

Jung's concept of the *Personal Shadow* is most closely aligned with Freud's notion of the "id" and represents the illicit desires, basic instincts, and selfish impulses repressed in our unconscious. We spend an inordinate amount of energy trying to deny, repress, or manage this aspect of being. We often explode in angry denial when someone points out a Shadow trait in our self that, while blatantly obvious to others, has been repressed. Jung reminded us that we do not become enlightened by pretending to be perfect; rather, we become enlightened when we're willing to confront and embrace this darker side of ourselves. This insight has key implications for the process of leadership development that will be discussed in our conclusion.

Finally, and most importantly for our purposes, is the concept of *Leadership Shadows*. We define them as the extreme and negative manifestation of our positive drivers, which are based on irrational thoughts, unfounded fears, and limiting core beliefs. Based on the three motive needs or drivers identified by McClelland, there are three *Leadership Shadows: Fear of Failure, Fear of Rejection,* and *Fear of Betrayal.* Table C.2 summarizes these shadows in the context of the ALP framework.

Table C.2. Leadership Shadows in the Context of the ALP Framework

Leadership Style	Leadership Shadow	Shadow Behaviors
Achiever	Fear of Failure	Micromanaging; obsessive; rigid; pessimistic; stubborn
Affirmer	Fear of Rejection	Conflict avoidant; devalues own opinions; accommodating
Asserter	Fear of Betrayal	Arrogant; controlling; skeptical; autocratic

However, when the Fear of Failure Leadership Shadow is activated, the strengths identified above become inherent limitations. Under stress, an Achiever will transform in unproductive ways: organized becomes rigid, detail-oriented devolves to being obsessive, and expertise leads to micromanagement. Much like Dr. Jekyll's transformation into Mr. Hyde, experiencing stress in the form of ambiguity or "losing" triggers the Fear of Failure Leadership Shadow, and the ugly transformation. The existential and ironic tragedy is that when this happens Achievers are actually more likely to fail.

The key contextual element related to all of the three styles and their corresponding Leadership Shadows is stress—that tense and taxing space we so often encounter in our professional and personal lives. This often results in career (and relationship) limiting moves, such as micromanaging, avoiding conflict, or refusing to trust others. And it is within this vicious cycle that we experience the tragedy of the human condition first identified by Frankl: paradoxical intent.

Abraham Maslow: Self-Actualization

Out of this somewhat dark and depressing state of the human condition came what is known today as the "Humanistic" movement in psychology led by Abraham Maslow and his concept of "self-actualization." As described earlier, prior to Maslow the vast majority of psychologists and researchers focused on human deficiencies: why people act in destructive or neurotic ways, for example. Maslow turned the field upside down when he began to focus on psychological health, well-being, and optimal performance. Maslow identified a number of characteristics and traits of these "self-actualizing" individuals that allow them to be more satisfied, more at peace, and ultimately, more effective. And what is perhaps most important to remember is that people aren't born this way. Just like the research into what causes or creates healthy cells in biology, Maslow found that there are changes we can make—both internally and externally in our environments—that facilitate and accelerate our growth and development.

Maslow's most famous contribution to the study of human behavior is his "Hierarchy of Needs" that attempts to explain human motivation from a needs-based and hierarchical perspective. According to Maslow (1954), there are four groups of basic or "deficiency" needs that must be met in ascending order. The goal of every individual is to meet a given need, and then allow a higher-order need to emerge to drive our behavior. Maslow illustrated, and many subsequent researchers have pointed out, that satisfying one need does not necessarily mean that a higher-order need will emerge. Both research and everyday experience demonstrate that many individuals get "stuck" in a certain deficiency need, for recognition or a sense of belonging to others, which can and does adversely impact one's ability for continued growth and development, which is the self-actualizing process. Figure C.1 provides an overview of Maslow's model, with the three motive needs captured in their appropriate level.

The four theoretical frameworks have been discussed in an attempt, albeit brief, to synthesize and integrate these into a

Figure C.1. Maslow's Hierarchy of Needs

comprehensive framework for the ALP. Next, this paper will examine the methodological approach for assessing the reliability and validity of the ALP and *Actualized Performance Cycle*. This examination will begin with a review of the scale development process, and the approach taken for the ALP.

THE SCALE DEVELOPMENT PROCESS

Designing and constructing an attitude assessment scale consists of three general stages: design, development, and evaluation (Schwab, 1980). The theoretical framework and literature review was presented to provide the general developmental foundation of the ALP. Within the three broad stages of constructing an attitude assessment scale, Hinkin (1998) identified six steps in the scale development process. These six steps are presented in Table C.3.

Item generation is the essential first step in developing a new Likert-type scale. The primary concern during this initial stage is content validity, which should be built into the scale through the development of clear, unambiguous, and accurate items that "adequately capture the specific domain of interest" (Hinkin, 1998).

It is during the initial design step that a researcher should understand the theoretical foundation that provides the basis for the scale's development. This study fell under the deductive approach to scale development because the theoretical foundation being used to define the ALP provided enough information to generate an initial

Table C.3. Six Steps in the Scale Development Process

Step 1:	Item Generation
Step 2:	Questionnaire Administration
Step 3:	Initial Item Reduction
Step 4:	Confirmatory Factor Analysis
Step 5:	Convergent/Discriminant Validity
Step 6:	Replication

set of items. The major advantage of the deductive approach to scale development is that, if done properly, this approach helps ensure content validity (Hinkin, 1995).

Survey administration is the second step of the Likert-type scale development process. During this stage of scale development, the items that were retained during the content validation assessment were administered to a pilot sample to confirm expectations of the psychometric properties of the new measure. Critical issues regarding scale development during this step included choosing a representative pilot sample, the sample size, and the total number of items in the new measure. These and other scaling issues are discussed in the reliability and validity sections of this paper.

Following the initial survey administration, the third step in the process of developing a Likert-type scale is the initial item reduction. Once preliminary data has been collected from the pilot sample, factor analysis was employed to further refine the scale. PCFA with orthogonal rotation is the most widely used factoring method for item reduction (Hinkin, 1995). Although no absolute cutoff exists for determining which items should remain on a given scale, that is which items most clearly represent the content domain of the underlying construct, a .40 criterion level is most commonly used to judge factor loadings as meaningful (Hinkin, 1998). PCFA was also used to determine the latent dimensions of the ALP framework, and a minimal eigenvalue of 1.0 was used as an appropriate criterion for retaining each dimension of the ALP assessment scale.

Once validity is established through PCFA, internal consistency should be established. Cronbach's alpha is the more widely accepted and utilized technique for establishing internal reliability, and is the recommended statistic when employing PCFA (Cortina, 1993).

The final two stages, assessing convergent and discriminant validity and replication, although critical to a scale's ultimate utility, are beyond the scope of this study. Convergent and discriminant validity are measures of criterion-related validity, the ability to predict a change in certain variables based on data from the predictor variable. Although this may be of eventual interest for the scale's utility, only face validity, content validity, and construct validity were ascertained for this investigation. Likewise, the final step, replication, is a time-consuming process that often takes years to establish (Hinkin, 1998). Preliminary data on replication reliability and validity will be gathered during the subsequent administrations of the ALP, as well as efforts to predict performance, job satisfaction, and intrinsic satisfaction (e.g., the correlation of Actualized Leader behaviors with individual and group performance, etc.). For the current investigation, validity was assessed using PCFA to determine both the underlying structure and the number of factors explaining the observed variance (eigenvalues ≥ 1.00), and PCFA was employed to determine survey item retention (≥ .40) for the five items per scale with the highest R^2.

Limitations of the Research Methodology

Likert-type scales offer a range of responses with different intensities from "strongly agree" to "strongly disagree." Each participant has a different interpretation of the response categories, which can lead to a degree of imprecision in the response set, data collection, and data analysis. Previous researchers have commented that Likert-type scales are akin to a "ruler that stretches or contracts," which can and does impact the precision of the data collected.

The study design has limited generalizability due to homogeneous samples used for data collection. Although the sample size is well beyond the recommended size of 200 (n=611), the sample was non-random and somewhat homogeneous (all members of the same organization). Additionally, the problems of social desirability and bias are limitations when using self-report measures. Social desirability, the tendency to answer questions in a manner the respondent believes that they should be answered, as opposed to the way the respondent actually believes, creates bias and error in the data analysis.

There are limitations related to validity as well. First and foremost, this research design does not afford a measure of criterion-related validity. Ultimately, one would want to be able to predict a group's performance based on the survey score. For example, are certain leadership styles, such as an Actualized Asserter, more effective than others with different challenges and tasks? Future research will need to establish criterion-related validity. Moreover, PCFA provides limited construct validity information due to the subjective nature of its statistical measures.

Study Sample Demographics

Before reviewing the validity and reliability analyses findings, the descriptive statistics for the current investigation are presented. First, the data was collected from a global, high-performance engineering and manufacturing company headquartered in Charlotte, NC, where, at the time of collection, the author was employed as the Vice President of Talent. The organization is a diversified company with six divisions that produces ball bearings, high performance sealants, submarine engines, and trailer solutions for the trucking industry.

Data for the survey administration sample were captured over a six (6) month period from October 2015 to March 2016. During this time, 611 participants completed the ALP as part of a larger leadership development program designed and facilitated within the study's host organization. Table C.4 summarizes the sample's demographics.

ASSESSING VALIDITY

Validity was assessed for the ALP using Principal Components Factor Analysis (PCFA), a statistical technique used for exploratory data analysis. The underlying assumption of exploratory data analysis is that the more one knows about the data, the more effectively and efficiently one can develop, test, and refine a given theory or, in this case, a measurement instrument (Hartwig & Dearing, 1979). Exploratory data analysis describes and summarizes data by grouping

Table C.4. Demographic Characteristics of Study Sample

Characteristic	Percentage (%)
Gender	
Male	68
Female	30
Missing Data	2
	100
Age	
20–30	10
31–40	30
41–50	42
51–60	9
61 and over	2
Missing Data	7
	100
Professional Experience	
1–5 Years	21
6–10 Years	22
11–15 Years	30
Over 15 Years	23
Missing Data	4
	100

together correlated variables in factors, labeled "components," that are independent of each other (Hartwig & Dearing, 1979). These components are often rotated to maximize the variance explained by each factor (Litwin, 1995).

Principal Components Factor Analysis

Principal Components Factor Analysis (PCFA) is a statistical technique that linearly transforms an original set of variables into a substantially smaller set of uncorrelated variables. This process identifies the relevant factors under study (Dunteman, 1989). PCFA is an appropriate statistical technique when the underlying factor structure is unknown. The goal of PCFA is data reduction, allowing the researcher to better understand and interpret data collected from a smaller set of uncorrelated variables (Dunteman, 1989).

There are several guidelines and requirements for using PCFA. There are numerous strategies for determining how many latent factors exist in a data set, and for ascertaining which survey items should be retained.

Assessing the Latent Structure of the Data Set

Determining the number of factors, or components, to retain depends on both the underlying theory and the quantitative results of the research endeavor (Hinkin, 1998). Several guidelines have been established to assist researchers in making decisions about the number of latent factors to retain.

Perhaps the most well-known rule of thumb in survey development is Kaiser's criterion. Kaiser's criterion (also known as Kaiser's Rule) states that only components with eigenvalues that are greater than 1.0 should qualify for retention. An eigenvalue is the total amount of variance explained by a factor, and it represents the sum of the squared loadings of each variable for that factor (Hinkin, 1998).

Another guide for determining the number of factors to retain in a PCFA is the scree plot test. The "scree" is defined as the rubble or valley where the graph plotting the factors begins to level off, and it is a graphically illustrated plot in the data set. As successive factors are extracted, and their contribution to explaining the observed variance decreases, the graph declines. The point of interest is where the curve connecting the points starts to flatten out. It is at this point where a valley or scree appears in the graph, and where factor retention may stop (Kinnear & Gray, 1999).

In addition to using the Kaiser criterion and scree plot test to decide on the number of factors to retain, the underlying theory or model guiding the research should also direct factor retention decisions so long as the data set is consistent with the model in use (Hinkin, 1998). That is, the research findings should fit the underlying theoretical framework in a conceptually sound way. The findings for the present study do fit the ALP framework and the conceptual models of human motivation as defined by McClelland (1987) and Maslow (1954), and a combination of the Kaiser criterion and the ALP theoretical framework was used to determine the number of latent factors to retain.

Latent Structure Assessment and Item Retention Analysis

PCFA of the measurement items was conducted from the data collected from the 611 surveys collected. An orthogonal (varimax) rotation was used to compute a loading matrix that represented the relationship between the observed variables and each factor. Initial PCFA statistics indicated the presence of four factors (i.e., components or dimensions of motive need leadership) with eigenvalues greater than 1.0 that accounted for 44.58% of the total variance observed (Table C.5). The remaining 55.32% of variance from the data set was not accounted for and was assumed to lie with factors not measured by the assessment instrument.

Table C.6 presents the eigenvalues by components and total variance explained by this analysis.

Variable (Item) Retention Analysis

Once the underlying structure of the data set has been determined, decisions surrounding which variables (i.e., survey items) to retain must be made. Although there is no universally accepted rule for the best way to determine which variables to retain, factor loadings computed by PCFA provide crucial information to assist the researcher (Hinkin, 1998). A factor loading is designated as a Pearson correlation coefficient of the original variable with the factor. Factor loadings range in value from +1.00, indicating a perfect positive association, to –1.00, which indicates a perfect negative association with the factor. It is generally agreed that in survey development, factor loadings of .40 or greater with no major cross-loading are deemed meaningful (Cattell, 1966; Hinkin, 1998; Nunnally, 1967). Variables usually load on all factors, but should load higher (.40 or greater) on only a single factor. Factor loadings and cross-loadings were considered in determining which items to retain in the final version of the Actualized Leader Profile, and the loadings for the retained items ranged from .510 to .792 (Table C.7).

The analyses used to determine which items were retained in the final version of the ALP were based on the factor loading scores solely, and in each instance (each component scale) the top five items with the highest factor loadings were selected for inclusion on the final version of the ALP. These scores, by component, follow in Table C.8.

Table C.5. PCFA Factors

Component 1	Power (Asserter Style)
Component 2	Affiliation (Affirmer Style)
Component 3	Achievement (Achiever Style)
Component 4	Self-Actualization (Actualized Style)

Table C.6. Total Variance Explained

Components	Initial Eigenvalues			Rotation Sums of Squared Loadings		
	Total	% of Variance	Cumulative %	Total	% of Variance	Cumulative %
1	14.131	28.262	28.262	6.426	12.853	12.853
2	3.420	6.840	35.101	5.308	10.616	23.469
3	2.831	5.663	40.764	5.189	10.377	33.846
4	1.906	3.812	44.576	3.563	7.126	40.971

Extraction Method: Principal Component Analysis

Table C.7. Scale Component Ranges

Achievement	.652–.584
Affiliation	.792–.563
Power	.792–.728
Self-Actualization	.632–.510

Table C.8. ALP Factor Loadings

Achievement Component Matrix	Component 3	Affiliation Component Matrix	Component 2	Power Component Matrix	Component 1	Self-Actualization Component Matrix	Component 4
wsb21	0.652	wsb35	0.792	wsb7	0.792	wsb18	0.632
wsb36	0.645	wsb11	0.731	wsb3	0.756	wsb10	0.562
wsb1	0.624	wsb6	0.73	wsb12	0.755	wsb27	0.53
wsb29	0.61	wsb2	0.649	wsb34	0.75	wsb24	0.525
wsb16	0.584	wsb19	0.563	wsb23	0.728	wsb8	0.51
wsb13	0.502	wsb22	0.488	wsb14	0.617	wsb32	0.498
wsb4	0.281	wsb37	0.455	wsb31	0.542	wsb5	0.489
wsb38	0.259	wsb25	0.231	wsb28	0.465	wsb33	0.483
wsb26	0.233	wsb30	0.161	wsb9	0.463	wsb15	0.421
wsb20	0.052	wsb17	0.161	wsb40	0.325	wsb39	0.18

Extraction Method: Principal Component Analysis.

ESTIMATING RELIABILITY

Coefficient alpha, commonly referred to as "Cronbach's alpha" and designated with "α," is a measure of internal consistency that estimates how well items "hang together." Reliability is a necessary condition for validity (Hinkin, 1998). In survey development, coefficient alpha measures the homogeneity of items for a given scale. Although there are other forms of reliability that can be estimated in survey research (Spector, 1992), coefficient alpha is a necessary estimate for scale development and the recommended reliability statistic when computing PCFA. The overall reliability estimates for each of the five scales of group culture are presented in Table C.9, and the specific statistical output for each scale follows. Reliability estimates were calculated for each scale of the Group Culture Assessment Scale in an iterative fashion. First, coefficient alphas were calculated for all 10 items of each scale. Then, internal consistency was estimated for the total number of items per scale to be retained in the survey's final version based on the PCFA assessment. The number of items retained for each scale in the survey's final version is five (5) per scale, using a minimum reliability estimate threshold of .40. The total number of items retained for this section of final version of the survey was 20. Table C.9 summarizes this reliability assessment effort utilizing Cronbach's alpha.

Table C.9. Reliability Assessment: Cronbach's Alpha

Scale	Cronbach's Alpha	Cronbach's Alpha Based on Standardized Items	N of Items
Achievement	0.864	0.857	5
Affiliation	0.783	0.781	5
Power	0.852	0.850	5
Self-Actualization	0.801	0.799	5

Reliability Assessment for the Achievement Scale

The Achievement scale possessed a total reliability of α = .864. Coefficient alpha was computed for the five (5) items retained for this scale. Item analysis indicated that the retained items had moderate to strong inter-item correlations ranging from .271 to .801 (Table C.10). The factor loadings (Table C.8) ranged from .584 to .652 (exceeding the .40 recommendation). Cronbach's alpha decreased if any of the items was deleted (Table C.11). The .40 minimum threshold established by Hinkin was used to make item retention decisions, although the actual reliability estimates for the retained items ranged from .506 to .838.

Reliability Assessment for the Affiliation Scale

The Affiliation scale possessed a total reliability of α = .783. Coefficient alpha was computed for the five (5) items retained for this scale. Item analysis indicated that the retained items had moderate to strong inter-item correlations ranging from .373 to .612 (Table C.12). The factor loadings (Table C.8) ranged from .563 to .792 (exceeding the .40 recommendation). Cronbach's alpha decreased if any of the items was deleted (Table C.13).

Reliability Assessment for the Power Scale

The Power scale possessed a total reliability of α = .852. Coefficient alpha was computed for the five (5) items retained for this scale. Item analysis indicated that the retained items had moderate to strong inter-item correlations ranging from .671 to .606 (Table C.14). The factor loadings (Table C.8) ranged from .728 to .792 (exceeding the .40 recommendation). Cronbach's alpha decreased if any of the items was deleted (Table C.15).

Reliability Assessment for the Self-Actualization Scale

The Self-Actualization scale possessed a total reliability of α = .801. Coefficient alpha was computed for the five (5) items retained for this scale. Item analysis indicated that the retained items had moderate

Table C.10. Achievement Scale: Inter-Item Correlation Matrix

	wsb4	wsb6	wsb9	wsb10	wsb20
wsb4	1.000	.575	.427	.739	.610
wsb6	.575	1.000	.271	.801	.784
wsb9	.427	.271	1.000	.482	.371
wsb10	.739	.801	.482	1.000	.817
wsb20	.610	.784	.371	.817	1.000

Table C.11. Achievement Scale: Item-Total Statistics

	Scale Mean if Item Deleted	Scale Variance if Item Deleted	Corrected Item-Total Correlation	Squared Multiple Correlation	Cronbach's Alpha if Item Deleted
wsb4	12.01	18.134	.708	.554	.861
wsb6	12.78	16.074	.770	.707	.847
wsb9	12.72	16.330	.800	.698	.838
wsb10	12.70	14.506	.904	.819	.810
wsb20	13.39	16.606	.818	.715	.834

Table C.12. Affiliation Scale: Inter-Item Correlation Matrix

	wsb8	wsb11	wsb13	wsb15	wsb18
wsb8	1.000	.387	.612	.483	.313
wsb11	.387	1.000	.373	.442	.406
wsb13	.612	.373	1.000	.575	.314
wsb15	.483	.442	.575	1.000	.262
wsb18	.313	.406	.314	.262	1.000

Table C.13. Affiliation Scale: Inter-Total Statistics

	Scale Mean if Item Deleted	Scale Variance if Item Deleted	Corrected Item-Total Correlation	Squared Multiple Correlation	Cronbach's Alpha if Item Deleted
wsb8	14.14	11.366	.613	.422	.725
wsb11	13.62	11.889	.531	.305	.751
wsb13	14.16	10.502	.645	.485	.712
wsb15	13.92	10.626	.599	.404	.729
wsb18	13.88	11.628	.572	.364	.738

Table C.14. Power Scale: Inter-Item Correlation Matrix

	wsb2	wsb3	wsb5	wsb16	wsb19
wsb2	1.000	.606	.603	.471	.571
wsb3	.606	1.000	.747	.519	.496
wsb5	.603	.747	1.000	.490	.552
wsb16	.471	.519	.490	1.000	.265
wsb19	.571	.496	.552	.265	1.000

Table C.15. Power Scale: Item-Total Statistics

	Scale Mean if Item Deleted	Scale Variance if Item Deleted	Corrected Item-Total Correlation	Squared Multiple Correlation	Cronbach's Alpha if Item Deleted
wsb2	13.35	13.623	.707	.507	.810
wsb3	12.85	12.999	.754	.616	.796
wsb5	13.10	12.711	.764	.624	.793
wsb16	13.25	15.230	.523	.329	.850
wsb19	13.76	14.323	.575	.404	.844

to strong inter-item correlations ranging from .253 to .649 (Table C.16). The factor loadings (Table C.8) ranged from .510 to .632 (exceeding the .40 recommendation). Cronbach's alpha decreased if any of the items was deleted (Table C.17).

In addition to the 20 retained survey items, there are 20 additional scale component (i.e., factor) words in 10 word-pairs that account for five (5) additional items per scale. This section of the ALP assessment scale requires the participant to choose the word from the word-pair that is most descriptive of him or her. When combined with the five (5) survey items per scale, this results in five (5) additional "items" (i.e., words) that impact the overall score of the participant. Cronbach's alphas for all five items were in the acceptable to good ranges (Table C.18.)

Reliability Assessment for the Word-Pair Achievement Scale

The Achievement scale possessed a total reliability of $\alpha = .755$. Coefficient alpha was computed for the five (5) items retained for

Table C.16. Self-Actualization Scale: Inter-Item Correlation Matrix

	wsb1	wsb7	wsb12	wsb14	wsb17
wsb1	1.000	.321	.253	.362	.330
wsb7	.321	1.000	.488	.465	.608
wsb12	.253	.488	1.000	.471	.478
wsb14	.362	.465	.471	1.000	.649
wsb17	.330	.608	.478	.649	1.000

Table C.17. Self-Actualization Scale: Item-Total Statistics

	Scale Mean if Item Deleted	Scale Variance if Item Deleted	Corrected Item-Total Correlation	Squared Multiple Correlation	Cronbach's Alpha if Item Deleted
wsb1	15.49	14.493	.394	.164	.796
wsb7	15.06	12.164	.627	.431	.750
wsb12	15.29	12.635	.553	.325	.774
wsb14	15.36	12.102	.652	.474	.742
wsb17	14.92	11.706	.703	.549	.724

Table C.18. Word Pairs: Cronbach's Alpha

Scale	Cronbach's Alpha	Cronbach's Alpha Based on Standardized Items	N of Items
Achievement	.755	.753	5
Affiliation	.818	.819	5
Power	.813	.810	5
Self-Actualization	.856	.830	5

this scale. Item analysis indicated that the retained items had moderate to strong inter-item correlations ranging from .331 to .551 (Table C.19). Cronbach's alpha decreased if any of the items was deleted (Table C.20).

Reliability Assessment for the Word-Pair Affiliation Scale

The Affiliation scale possessed a total reliability of α = .818. Coefficient alpha was computed for the five (5) items retained for this scale. Item analysis indicated that the retained items had

Table C.19. Word-Pair Achievement Scale: Inter-Item Correlation Matrix

	winning	reserved	expertise	perfection	tactical
winning	1.000	.423	.408	.331	.190
reserved	.423	1.000	.551	.471	.302
expertise	.408	.551	1.000	.428	.373
perfection	.331	.471	.428	1.000	.279
tactical	.190	.302	.373	.279	1.000

Table C.20. Word-Pair Achievement Scale: Item-Total Statistics

	Scale Mean if Item Deleted	Scale Variance if Item Deleted	Corrected Item-Total Correlation	Squared Multiple Correlation	Cronbach's Alpha if Item Deleted
winning	13.95	195.212	.460	.234	.731
reserved	14.41	180.523	.622	.404	.671
expertise	13.32	174.542	.622	.400	.669
perfection	13.39	186.000	.520	.282	.709
tactical	15.42	217.192	.378	.163	.754

moderate to strong inter-item correlations ranging from .411 to .609 (Table C.21). Cronbach's alpha decreased if any of the items was deleted (Table C.22).

Reliability Assessment for the Word-Pair Power Scale

The Power scale possessed a total reliability of $\alpha = .813$. Coefficient alpha was computed for the five (5) items retained for this scale. Item analysis indicated that the retained items had moderate to strong inter-item correlations ranging from .172 to .771 (Table C.23). Cronbach's alpha decreased if any of the items was deleted (Table C.24).

Reliability Assessment for the Word-Pair Self-Actualization Scale

The Self-Actualization scale possessed a total reliability of $\alpha = .856$. Coefficient alpha was computed for the five (5) items retained for this scale. Item analysis indicated that the retained items had

Table C.21. Word-Pair Affiliation Scale: Inter-Item Correlation Matrix

	empathy	relationships	caring	warm	mercy
empathy	1.000	.580	.542	.429	.411
relationships	.580	1.000	.609	.497	.454
caring	.542	.609	1.000	.460	.436
warm	.429	.497	.460	1.000	.324
mercy	.411	.454	.436	.324	1.000

Table C.22. Word-Pair Affiliation Scale: Item-Total Statistics

	Scale Mean if Item Deleted	Scale Variance if Item Deleted	Corrected Item-Total Correlation	Squared Multiple Correlation	Cronbach's Alpha if Item Deleted
empathy	24.26	223.474	.634	.416	.775
relationships	24.57	212.902	.705	.507	.753
caring	24.34	218.896	.668	.459	.764
warm	24.39	234.067	.538	.303	.802
mercy	26.08	232.754	.508	.266	.812

Table C.23. Word-Pair Power Scale: Inter-Item Correlation Matrix

	justice	strategic	power	control	results
justice	1.000	.370	.388	.588	.771
strategic	.370	1.000	.172	.229	.464
power	.388	.172	1.000	.248	.362
control	.588	.229	.248	1.000	.647
results	.771	.464	.362	.647	1.000

Table C.24. Word-Pair Power Scale: Item-Total Statistics

	Scale Mean if Item Deleted	Scale Variance if Item Deleted	Corrected Item-Total Correlation	Squared Multiple Correlation	Cronbach's Alpha if Item Deleted
justice	18.40	183.938	.743	.621	.694
strategic	16.97	230.472	.395	.226	.809
power	21.64	248.358	.369	.160	.810
control	18.28	202.505	.579	.445	.753
results	18.99	177.882	.805	.690	.671

moderate to strong inter-item correlations ranging from .123 to .828 (Table C.25). Cronbach's alpha decreased if any of the items was deleted (Table C.26).

Table C.25. Word-Pair Self-Actualization Scale: Inter-Item Correlation Matrix

	risk	spontaneous	candor	trust	creativity
risk	1.000	.828	.378	.254	.746
spontaneous	.828	1.000	.425	.266	.780
candor	.378	.425	1.000	.123	.342
trust	.254	.266	.123	1.000	.114
creativity	.746	.780	.342	.114	1.000

Table C.26. Word-Pair Self-Actualization Scale: Item-Total Statistics

	Scale Mean if Item Deleted	Scale Variance if Item Deleted	Corrected Item-Total Correlation	Squared Multiple Correlation	Cronbach's Alpha if Item Deleted
risk	22.10	166.280	.812	.717	.673
spontaneous	21.92	161.801	.856	.767	.655
candor	23.26	222.064	.359	.246	.825
trust	17.80	270.319	.157	.173	.851
creativity	21.86	174.476	.728	.653	.704

SUMMARY

The Actualized Leader Profile is a valid and reliable self-report assessment for measuring human motivation and leader style, based on the integrated framework resulting from combining the Acquired Needs Theory (McClelland, 1987) and self-actualization (Maslow, 1954). The steps outlined in this effort follow well-accepted guidelines for the scale development process (Hinkin, 1995) and yield a four-factor model of human behavior and leader style, with impressive factor loading well above the suggested .40 cutoff, indicating that the retained survey items assess their desired component as defined in the theoretical framework. Moreover, the scales are estimated to have a high degree of reliability. The scales' average Cronbach's alpha is .818, meaning that the consistency of the items by scale is good. As such, it can be affirmed that the Actualized Leader Profile is both a precise (valid) and consistent (reliable) assessment for measuring leader style, based on the underlying motive needs of the participant.

References

Alderfer, Clayton P. 1972. *Existence, Relatedness, and Growth: Human Needs in Organizational Settings.* New York: Free Press.

Bion, Wilfred R. 1961. *Experiences in Groups: And Other Papers.* New York: Basic Books.

Blake, Robert R. and Jane S. Mouton. 1968. *The Managerial Grid: Key Orientations for Achieving Production Through People.* Houston, TX: Gulf Publishing.

Blanchard, Kenneth, Patricia Zigarmi, and Drea Zigarmi. 1999. *Leadership and The One Minute Manager: Increasing Effectiveness Through Situational Leadership.* New York: William Morrow.

Brach, Tara. 2003. *Radical Acceptance: Embracing Your Life with the Heart of a Buddha.* New York: Bantam Dell.

Brookings Institution. 2015. *Opportunity, Responsibility, and Security: A Consensus Plan for Reducing Poverty and Restoring the American Dream.* Washington, DC: AEI/Brookings.

Brown, Brené. 2012a. *Daring Greatly: How the Courage to Be Vulnerable Transforms the Way We Live, Love, Parent, and Lead.* New York: Gotham Books.

———. 2012b. *The Power of Vulnerability: Teachings on Authenticity, Connection, and Courage.* Read by the author. Louisville, CO: Sounds True.

Browning, Peter C., and William L. Sparks. 2016. *The Director's Manual: A Framework for Board Governance.* Hoboken, NJ: Wiley.

Byrne, Rhonda. 2006. *The Secret.* New York: Atria Books.

Cattell, Raymond B. "The Scree Test for the Number of Factors." *Multivariate Behavioral Research* 1, no. 2 (April 1966): 245–76.

Chambers, John. 2016. "Cisco's John Chambers on the Digital Era." Interview by Rik Kirkland. *McKinsey Quarterly* 2016, no. 2. https://www.mckinsey.com/industries/high-tech/our-insights/ciscos-john-chambers-on-the-digital-era.

Collins, Jim. 2001. *Good to Great: Why Some Companies Make the Leap . . . and Others Don't.* New York: HarperBusiness.

Cortina, Jose M. "What is Coefficient Alpha?: An Examination of Theory and Applications." *Journal of Applied Psychology* 78, no. 1 (February 1993): 98–104.

Covey, Stephen R. 1990. *The 7 Habits of Highly Effective People: Powerful Lessons in Personal Change.* New York: Free Press.

Csikszentmihalyi, Mihaly. 2008. *Flow: The Psychology of Optimal Experience.* New York: Harper Perennial Modern Classics.

Dame, John and Jeffrey Gedmin. "Six Principles for Developing Humility as a Leader." *Harvard Business Review*, September 2013. https://hbr.org/2013/09/six-principles-for-developing.

De Angelis, Barbara. 2007. *How Did I Get Here? Finding Your Way to Renewed Hope and Happiness When Life and Love Take Unexpected Turns.* New York: St. Martin's Press.

De Becker, Gavin. 1995. *The Gift of Fear: Survival Signals That Protect Us from Violence.* New York: Dell Publishing.

Devine, CaSondra and William L. Sparks. "Defining Moments: Toward a Comprehensive Theory of Personal Transformation." *International Journal of Humanities and Social Science* 4, no. 5(1) (March 2014): 31–39.

Drucker, Peter F. 2008. *The Essential Drucker: In One Volume the Best of Sixty Years of Peter Drucker's Essential Writings on Management.* New York: HarperBusiness.

Dunteman, George H. 1989. *Principal Components Analysis.* Newbury Park, CA: Sage Publications, Inc.

Dweck, Carol S. 2006. *Mindset: The New Psychology of Success.* New York: Random House.

Enright, Robert. 2001. *Forgiveness is a Choice.* Washington, DC: American Psychological Association.

Frankl, Viktor E. 1959. *Man's Search for Meaning.* Boston: Beacon Press.

Fromm, Erich. 1994. *Escape from Freedom.* New York: Holt Paperbacks.

Gilbert, Elizabeth. 2016. *Big Magic: Creative Living Beyond Fear.* New York: Riverhead Books.

Goleman, Daniel. 1995. *Emotional Intelligence: Why It Can Matter More Than IQ.* New York: Bantam Books.

———. 2015. *Focus: The Hidden Driver of Excellence.* New York: Harper Paperbacks.

Goleman, Daniel, Richard Boyatzis, and Annie McKee. 2002. *Primal Leadership: Learning to Lead with Emotional Intelligence.* Boston: Harvard Business School Press.

Hartwig, Frederick and Brian E. Dearing. 1979. *Exploratory Data Analysis.* Newbury Park, CA: Sage Publications, Inc.

Harvey, Jerry B. 1988. *The Abilene Paradox: And Other Meditations on Management.* San Francisco: Jossey-Bass.

———. 1999. *How Come Every Time I Get Stabbed in the Back My Fingerprints Are on the Knife? And Other Meditations on Management.* San Francisco: Jossey-Bass.

Helgoe, Laurie. 2013. *Introvert Power: Why Your Inner Life is Your Hidden Strength*. Naperville, IL: Sourcebooks.

Hersey, Paul. 1985. *The Situational Leader: The Other 59 Minutes*. New York: Warner Books.

Herzberg, Frederick, Bernard Mausner, and Barbara Bloch Snyderman. 1959. *The Motivation to Work*. New Brunswick, NJ: Transaction Publishers.

Hill, Napoleon. 2005. *Think and Grow Rich*. New York: TarcherPerigree.

Hinkin, Timothy R. 1995. "A Review of Scale Development Practices in the Study of Organizations." *Journal of Management* 21, no. 5 (1995): 967–86.

———. 1998. "A Brief Tutorial on the Development of Measures for Use in Survey Questionnaires." *Organizational Research Methods* 1, no. 1 (1998): 104–21.

Howard, Pierce J. 2013. *The Owner's Manual for Happiness: Essential Elements of a Meaningful Life*. Charlotte, NC: CentACS.

Howard, Pierce J. and Jane Mitchell Howard. 2000. *The Owner's Manual for Personality at Work: How the Big Five Personality Traits Affect Your Performance, Communication, Teamwork, Leadership, and Sales*. Austin, TX: Bard Press.

Ioannou, Lori. 2014. "A Decade to Mass Extinction Event in S&P 500." CNBC, June 5, 2014. https://www.cnbc.com/2014/06/04/15-years-to-extinction-sp-500-companies.html.

Judge, Timothy A., Chad A. Higgins, Carl J. Thoresen, and Murray R. Barrick. 1999. "The Big Five Personality Traits, General Mental Ability, and Career Success Across the Life Span." *Personnel Psychology* 52, no. 3 (September): 621–52.

Jung, C.G. 1927. The Structure of the Psyche. Vol. 8, Collected Works. London: Routledge & Kegan Paul; Princeton: Princeton University Press.

———. 1963. *Memories, Dreams, Reflections.* New York: Pantheon.

———. 1964. *Man and His Symbols.* Garden City, NY: Doubleday.

———. 1969. *The Structure and Dynamics of the Psyche.* 2nd ed. Princeton, NJ: Princeton University Press.

———. 1976. *The Portable Jung.* New York: Penguin Classics.

———. (1989) 2014. *Essays on Contemporary Events: The Psychology of Nazism.* Reprint, Princeton, NJ: Princeton University Press.

Kinnear, Paul R. and Colin D. Gray. 1999. *SPSS for Windows Made Simple.* 3rd ed. East Sussex, UK: Psychology Press Ltd., Publishers.

Kotler, Steven. 2014. *The Rise of Superman: Decoding the Science of Ultimate Human Performance.* London: Quercus.

Kriegel, Robert J. and Louis Patler. 1992. *If It Ain't Broke . . . Break It! And Other Unconventional Wisdom for a Changing Business World.* New York: Warner Books.

Lewis, C. S. 1960. *The Four Loves.* New York: Harcourt, Brace.

Litwin, Mark S., ed. 1995. *How to Measure Survey Reliability and Validity. Vol. 7, The Survey Kit,* edited by Arlene Fink. Thousand Oaks, CA: Sage Publications, Inc.

Lyubomirsky, Sonja. 2007. *The How of Happiness: A New Approach to Getting the Life You Want.* New York: Penguin Press.

Maccoby, Eleanor E. 2000. *The Two Sexes: Growing Up Apart, Coming Together.* Cambridge, MA: Harvard University Press.

Maraboli, Steve. 2009. *Life, the Truth, and Being Free.* Port Washington, NY: A Better Today.

Maslow, A. H. 1954. *Motivation and Personality.* New York: Harper.

———. 1987. *Motivation and Personality.* 3rd edition. New York: HarperCollins.

———. 1993. *The Farther Reaches of Human Nature.* New York: Penguin/Arkana.

———. 1998. *Toward a Psychology of Being.* 3rd edition. Hoboken, NJ: Wiley.

McClelland, David C. 1988. *Human Motivation.* Cambridge: Cambridge University Press.

Myers, Isabel Briggs with Peter B. Myers. 1995. *Gifts Differing: Understanding Personality Type.* Mountain View, CA: Davies-Black.

Newport, Cal. 2016. *Deep Work: Rules for Focused Success in a Distracted World.* New York: Grand Central.

Niebuhr, Reinhold. 1987. *The Essential Reinhold Niebuhr: Selected Essays and Addresses.* Edited by Robert McAfee Brown. New Haven, CT: Yale University Press.

Nunnally, Jum C. 1967. *Psychometric Theory.* New York: McGraw-Hill.

Porter, Michael E. "What is Strategy?" *Harvard Business Review* 74, no. 6 (November–December 1996): 61–78.

Privette, Gayle. 2001. "Defining Moments of Self-Actualization: Peak Performance and Peak Experience." In *The Handbook of Humanistic Psychology: Leading Edges in Theory, Research, and Practice,* edited by Kirk J. Schneider, James F. T. Bugental, and J. Fraser Pierson, 161–77. Thousand Oaks, CA: Sage.

Richo, David. 2005. *The Five Things We Cannot Change . . . and the Happiness We Find by Embracing Them*. Boston: Shambhala.

Robbins, Stephen P. and Mary A. Coulter. 2011. *Management*. 11th ed. Upper Saddle River, NJ: Prentice Hall.

Schwab, Donald P. 1980. "Construct Validity in Organizational Behavior." In vol. 2 of *Research in Organizational Behavior*, edited by Larry L. Cummings and Barry M. Straw. Greenwich, CT: JAI.

Schwartzberg, Louie. 2011. "Nature. Beauty. Gratitude." Filmed June 2011 in San Francisco, CA. TED video, 9:40. https://www.ted.com/talks/louie_schwartzberg_nature_beauty_gratitude.

Siegel, Daniel J. 2010. *Mindsight: The New Science of Personal Transformation*. New York: Bantam Books.

Sparks, William L. "Measuring the Impact of Basic Assumption Mental States on Group Culture: The Design, Development and Evaluation of the Group Culture Assessment Scale." Unpublished doctoral dissertation, 2002.

Spector, Paul E. 1992. *Summated Rating Scale Construction: An Introduction*. Newbury Park, CA: Sage Publications, Inc.

Spreier, Scott, Mary H. Fontaine, and Ruth Malloy. "Leadership Run Amok: The Destructive Potential of Overachievers." *Harvard Business Review* 84, no. 6 (June 2006): 72–82.

Tolle, Eckhart. 2004. *The Power of Now: A Guide to Spiritual Enlightenment*. Vancouver, BC: Namaste.

Waldman, David A. and David E. Bowen. 2016. "Learning to Be a Paradox-Savvy Leader." *Academy of Management Perspectives* 30, no. 3 (August): 316–27.

Welch, Jack. 2005. *Winning*. New York: HarperBusiness.

Index

Asserters (continued)
   and dependent group culture 53
   and Fear of Betrayal leadership
      shadow 45. *See also* power
   and trust 79

assurance 128–132. *See also* Fear of Betrayal
leadership shadow

B

Bacon, Francis 63

basic assumption states (BAMS) 47

Bessant, Catherine B. 89, 90

Big Magic 92

Bion, Wilfred 46

Blake, Robert 21

Blanchard, Ken 22

Brach, Tara 83–84, 109

Briggs Myers, Isabel 109

Brookings Institution 134

Brown, Brené 77, 129–130, 135

Browning, Peter 140

Brown, Jeffrey J. 70

burnout 103

Byrne, Rhonda 18

C

Campbell, Joseph 147

candor 88, 104

cognitive behavioral therapy (CBT) 37–38,
60
   and leadership shadows 41–43
   and the Actualized Leader Profile
     (ALP) 38–45

collective unconscious 29. *See also* shadow;
collective

Collins, Jim 62, 89, 140

Confidence Sequence of self-
actualization 102, 103–105. *See
also* candor; courage; objectivity

connection 125–128. *See also* Fear of
Rejection leadership shadow

conscientiousness 48

courage 74–77, 104

Covey, Stephen
   and objectivity 62–63
   and response-ability 34
   and solitude 97
   and the Obituary Exercise 148
   and the Renewal Sequence of
     self-actualization 110

Csikszentmihalyi, Mihaly 22, 92, 106

Curry, Michael B. 76, 102

D

Dame, John 140

Davies, Pamela S. 95

De Angelis, Barbara 119

de Becker, Gavin 75

Deep Work 65

dependency 6–7

Director's Manual, The 50

Drucker, Peter 18

Dweck, Carol 122, 124

E

Eat Pray Love 92

Emerson, Ralph Waldo 147

Emotional Intelligence 18

emotional intelligence (EI/EQ) 43, 73

Epictetus 42

Escape from Freedom 133

eudaimonia 92. *See also* flow

extroversion 28, 48

F

Fear of Betrayal leadership shadow 45
   and assurance 128–132

Fear of Failure leadership shadow 44
   and abundance 122–123

Fear of Rejection leadership shadow 44
   and connection 125–128

Five Things We Cannot Change, The 143

fixed mindset 122. *See also* scarcity

flow 22, 63, 91–100, 106

Focus: The Hidden Driver of Excellence 66

About the Author

William L. Sparks serves as the Dennis Thompson Chair and Professor of Leadership at the McColl School of Business at Queens University of Charlotte. Concurrently, he serves as the Managing Partner with William L. Sparks & Associates, LLC, and as a Partner with Peter Browning Partners, LLC, providing leadership, team, and board development services to organizations worldwide. He created and validated the Actualized Leader Profile©, the ALP360©, and the Actualized Team Profile© over the last twenty years, and they have been translated into nine languages. His TEDx Talk, "The Power of Self-Awareness," explores the importance of personal responsibility for self-actualization. He completed his Ph.D. in Organizational Behavior and Development from the School of Business and Public Management at the George Washington University.